CW00765044

THE GIRL FROM
GUILDFORD
STREET

THE GIRL FROM GUILDFORD STREET

Growing up in working class
Birmingham 1957–1968

Grace Caroline Holte

BREWIN BOOKS

BREWIN BOOKS
56 Alcester Road,
Studley,
Warwickshire,
B80 7LG
www.brewinbooks.com

Published by Brewin Books 2018

A CIP catalogue record for this book is available from the
British Library.

ISBN: 978-1-85858-579-6

Printed and bound in Great Britain
by Severn Print Ltd.

Contents

This book is dedicated to my parents and my grandmother and also for my sister Susannah Leigh and David and Mark, my cousins, the only ones left who remember what it was like to be the last generation of children growing up in the back to backs.

Cast of Characters

Our Family – no 37
Dad (Bill)
Mom (Lil)
Grace (b. 1957), *Susannah* (b. 1958), daughters

2 back of 37
Elsie (Nan)
Uncle Bill, who later marries *Auntie Margaret* and moves to Sutton
  Coldfield.
Uncle John, who marries *Auntie June*.
Uncle Charlie, who marries *Auntie Ann* and moves to Bearwood. Parents of
  my cousin *Marie*.
Auntie Eileen, who marries *Uncle Bernard* and moves to Solihull. Parents of
  my cousins *Dean* and *Tracey*.
Great Auntie Lil, Nan's sister and *Great Uncle Jack*.
Great Aunt Ada, Nan's sister.
Great Uncle Fred and *Great Aunt Minnie,* parents of Mom's cousins, *Gill* and
  Hazel.

35 next to 37
Great Aunt Floss, Mom's aunt and her husband, our *Great Uncle Bertie*.
David and *Mark,* their sons and our cousins.

Neighbours – *Cherie Luttrell* (no 39), friend and neighbour, the Etkins
  family (no 33).

Dad's family
Uncle Albert, his brother and *Auntie Mary*, parents of my cousins *Jim* and
  Janet.
Uncle Charlie, his brother, and *Auntie Lil*, parents of *John* and my step
  cousins *Maureen* and *Eileen*.

Auntie Jean and *Uncle Ray*
Uncle John and *Auntie Jean*

At William Cowper

Mr Sims, headmaster of the Juniors. Miss Cope, headmistress of the
 Infants. Mrs Wardell, Secretary. The teachers: Miss Reeve. Miss Reid, Mr
 Ellis, Mr Webb, Young Mr Jones, Big Mr Jones, Miss Jones (Mrs Francis),
 Mrs Burton, Mr Tapper, Mr Hindle.

Friends: Sandra Steele, Philip Hart, Alan Lea, Ronnie Hassan, Linda
 Broadfield (Ramsey).

Family Friends

Stan and *Barbara Atkins* and their children *Lynne* and *Andrew*
Pat and *John (Sean) Bowman*
Roy 'Mac' McManus and *Doreen*
Harold and *Claire Styles*
Jim and *Phil Grogan*
John and *Nora Nevin* and son *Johnnie*
Frank and *Elsie Collins* and daughters *Marie* and *Vanessa*
Johnnie (Sean) Murray, Dad's friend and right hand man at Tucker
 Fasteners; married to *Maureen*

Dr Carolan, family GP

I'd give all the wealth that years have piled,
The slow result of life's decay,
To be once more a little child
for one bright summer day.

Lewis Carroll

So sad, so sweet, the days that are no more.

Alfred Lord Tennyson, *Tears, idle Tears*

Golden lads and girls all must,
As chimney sweepers, come to dust.

William Shakespeare, *Cymbeline*

Introduction

"How lucky you are," said my students, "to be a child of the Sixties?"

It was shortly after my mother died, in 2015. In a moment of nostalgia, the week after her death, I changed the subject of my English class; instead of Romantic poetry, we would look at Lennon/McCartney lyrics, the music of my childhood. And why not? The Americans value the lyrics of Bob Dylan.

We were looking at the lyrics of "She's Leaving Home" and "Eleanor Rigby", because they had been favourites of my father.

"How can such young men know such things?" he would ask, as he listened to them on the radio – the radio which was on every day in my parents' home, permanently tuned to the Light Programme (never the Home Service or the Third Programme, the only other radio services available to us, till as a teenager, I discovered Radios Caroline and Luxembourg).

My students, as it turned out, had an idealized view of the Sixties.

"The clothes and the hairstyles were lovely," said a fashion design student.

"And the music was wonderful," said one of the music tech lads.

"We had the greatest car industry in the world, and almost full employment," said a student studying automotives.

"And most of all, it's the important political acts," said a student studying politics. "You know, Equal Pay for Women, and the decriminalisation of homosexuality, and the relaxation of censorship on the stage, that sort of thing."

A teacher training student said:

"It's the decade when working class students begin to go to University 'cos there's a grants system, and there's the birth of the Open University."

They looked at me expectantly.

"It's not what I remember," I said. "I was a child *in* the Sixties; I wasn't a child *of* the Sixties."

When my mother died, I spent hours sorting through boxes of family memorabilia. I was surprised at what she had kept, preserved. There were albums of photographs going back to 1900, but most touching to me were the photographs dating back to 1957, the year I was born. In 1970, the family photographs burst into glorious colour, but before that, they are black and white, like our twelve inch screen black and white TV. Life in black and white, as it does indeed seem when you are a child.

My father had left folders and folders of family history research. He had taken to doing family history when he retired at the age of 64, after 40 years working in a factory. He did it, as he did all things, well. I had not realised how thorough his research had been – generations of nameless, faceless ancestors suddenly sprung to life.

Tears came to my eyes as I put the folders and albums down, and I thought:

"They don't deserve to be forgotten. Their story ought to be written down."

This is the story of a happy childhood, 1957 – 1968, and when I say happy, I don't mean that I lived a privileged, idealized childhood. I was the child of two working class Birmingham factory workers, and we lived in a two bedroom back to back with no central heating or running hot water, and an outside toilet. Yet we were supremely happy in the way that only a child can be.

1. Mom and Her Family

When my father develops an interest in family history late in life, he offers to research the history of my mother's family.

"I don't want that," she says ominously. "All sort of things might come to life."

So everything I hear of my mother's family is hearsay, what she tells us. She is born in 1930 in Aston, the eldest child of William and Elsie. Her brother William (Billy) follows in 1932, and a short lived sister, Eileen, in 1937.

"Oh she was beautiful," says my mother many years later. "Black curly hair, and big dark eyes." She has one, tiny blurred photograph of her sitting up in a pram.

"I remember the night she died. She hadn't been well, and your nan said to me, 'Put the bab up to bed'. I carried her up and put her down, and then I saw she wasn't breathing. I screamed out to Nan and Billy, he ran for the doctor. But when the doctor came, he said, 'She's gone, Mrs Palfrey'."

The doctor writes 'Cause of death: pneumonia' on the death certificate. My grandfather is at war – he joined up on the day war broke out in 1939 – and so on Christmas Eve, 1940, my nan goes to Eileen's funeral all by herself. She is buried in a common grave for babies as my nan cannot afford to buy a grave.

My mother does not speak very much of her childhood. It is spent in 2 back of 37 Guildford St, the house my nan came to as a bride, and never leaves till 1968, two years before she dies.

My mother has three grandparents, Granny Palfrey, and Nan and Grandad Hatfield, Elsie's parents.

"Granny Palfrey was a bit of a tartar," says my mother. "Everyone feared her."

Still, she says defensively, Granny Palfrey was very good to her, and she has had a hard life; she was widowed in the Twenties, and had to bring up four children alone. These are my grandad, my great uncle Tom, my great uncle Fred, and my great aunt Floss.

I think she prefers her other gran, Granny Hatfield.

"She has a mass of long hair and she used to let me put her hair into a big bun, and she would say, 'Oh, our Lily!'"

Nan and Grandad Hatfield have four children – Bill, Elsie, and my great aunts Ada and Lil.

My mother is named Lilian Emily for her two grandmothers, but she doesn't like her names. All the girls in the family have the same names passed from generation to generation: Lilian, Emily, Ada, Florence, Nancy, Annie, Ellen or Nell – names which have become curiously fashionable.

My mother does not have such happy memories of her Grandad Hatfield.

"He wouldn't let Gran smoke," she says. "Gran would have a cigarette, while he was down at the pub, and then she would open all the windows, and say, 'Our Lily, help me get all the smoke out'."

The pub, is of course, the preserve of the white working-class male, and all the pubs in Aston have frosted glass windows or curtains up so that women and children can't look in and observe the proceedings. We have got lots of pubs, Victorian gin palaces with Minto tiles, stained glass windows and polished wood fittings: the Bartons Arms, the Clement, the Holte Arms.

My nan only speaks of her dad once.

"I had my hair bobbed in 1928," she says. "I went into Birmingham and had it done and then I went to Dubarry's Photographic Studio and had my photo taken."

She shows me and my sister the photograph – she gazes out from under a fashionable fringe, the bob reaching just under her ears.

"Well, after that, I didn't go home because I was frightened of what your great grandad would say. Your great gran had to wear her hair long because that was what he liked. And when I got home, Dad, he started to shout. But your great uncle, my brother Bill, he stood up for me, and he said, "You leave that girl alone.""

Like all her family, my nan left school at the age of fourteen. Her school leaving certificate still survives, a battered piece of paper dating from 1920. It tells the world that Elsie is a good girl, punctual and polite, quick in her studies. It doesn't in fact matter how good Elsie is at school; like all the women of her family, she goes straight into the factories when she leaves school, where she will do the same work as the men and for less pay. No nonsense here about the weaker sex then.

All of my family have always worked in the factories of Birmingham; before that, they were agricultural labourers. They work for long hours in back breaking toil; no sick leave, no annual leave, no pension. My father traces the death certificates, the parish entries for some of them; exhaustion, it says over and over, as cause of death.

My mother adores her father, who is a bricklayer. She is the first person he confides in when he joins up in 1939.

"Don't tell anyone," he says, as though they might not find out.

He dies in 1942, not in action, but of pneumonia at Barry Island training camp. He was in the Royal Engineers at Dunkirk, and spent hours in freezing water, building floating piers and ramps. My mother says she can remember the telegram coming, and my nan rushing out into the street in her nightdress. That is as much as she will ever say; she can never speak of her father without weeping.

She says that her father's body was brought home; that he had a bandage around his head; that he lay in state in the living room in the days before the funeral; that he had a magnificent funeral with six black horses with plumes drawing the coffin; that people came out to line the streets of Aston as he is driven to Witton Cemetery. I find that difficult to believe; my grandmother had no money for a lavish funeral. Yet she certainly spent £15 to purchase a grave for him; I have the deeds to it still, dated 1942.

My grandmother receives a war widow's pension, but she loses it when she remarries in 1944, someone she met down at the pub, a Charlie Knowles, a widower, who works in the munitions factory. His wife died in childbirth in 1939. She also acquires two stepchildren, my step aunt and uncle, Eileen and Charlie. Now six people are crowded into a council two up one down; the children in one bedroom and the parents in another. It becomes seven when my nan gives birth to another son, John.

Nan's second husband dies in 1944. She arranges her third funeral. I always think that she goes home that night and puts the children to bed. From that time on, Bill, Charlie and John sleep in one bedroom, and she shares the other with my mother and Eileen. She drinks a cup of tea as she sits at the table and takes stock. She is now thirty-six, twice married, and lives in a council house two up and one down with an outside toilet and no bathroom. She has no visible means of income. She has three children, two stepchildren, a dead daughter and two dead husbands. They have left her nothing at all. She dreads the stigma of social services, of getting them involved; she will not go to the church or the parish and beg.

I think she decides that from now on, she will do it all by herself; no more marriages. My mother is fourteen and will need to leave school. My mother is bright, literate and numerate; she can add up in her head. She will never need a calculator in her entire life. She can tell the cashier the total of her shopping bill before the cashier even starts inputting. At school she has always sat on the Top Bench. She receives a glowing school leaving report from her headmistress at Lozells County Secondary School. Her father had intended her to stay on at school, to go to college, to do bookkeeping. But now she must leave and support the rest of the family. She is fourteen; "go out", says my grandmother, "and walk around all the factories till you find a job."

"Bill shouldn't have joined up," says my great aunt Floss many years later. "It changed the lives of the whole family."

There are few options for the women of my family. A few, like my aunts Jean and Margaret, will get themselves a job in a hairdressing salon when they leave school; they will sweep up, wash tea cups, and study for their City and Guilds at night school or college. My step aunt, Eileen, will manage to get herself, with the help of money from her grandparents, an office job, while she studies typing and shorthand and bookkeeping at college. But for the majority of women in my family there is no choice. At the age of fourteen, into the factories they will go. They will stay there till they get married and have children, when they will promptly lose their jobs, as there is no maternity pay or childcare. They will do the same job, heavy and demanding, as the men, for less pay.

In fact, my mother's first job is in Birmingham's famous Jewellery Quarter. The Jewellery Quarter is no longer making jewellery; there's a war on and they are making munitions. My mother makes parts for helmets. She doesn't stay there long; she has started going to the local Youth Club at Burlington Hall, which is run by the Quakers, and the Leader gives her a letter of introduction to Cadbury's Chocolate Factory. This will mean either catching two buses from Lozells, or catching a train from Aston to Bournville, but it's well known that Cadbury's are Birmingham's best employer. My mother is hired as a trainee chocolatier, and as an added bonus she brings home bags of seconds and misshapes. Cadbury's are quick to spot her potential; she is put on a quality control training scheme.

My family have very little interest in the war; life is a personal battle to survive. My nan has already refused to have the children evacuated; if they die, they die together, she says. The back yard has an air raid shelter, but she never uses it; she just makes a pot of tea when the air raid sirens sound, and sits drinking it at the table. Her brother in law, Uncle Jack, Aunty Lily's husband, works for the council, and has got her some light cleaning jobs at the Law Courts and at Aston Library, which she can do very early in the morning or late at night; she walks to both of them. Birmingham is of course battered by the Luftwaffe; they are going for the factories, and they often hit the terraced homes of the thousands of working class people who live next to them. My parents are now buried close to the tombstone of an entire family, parents and two children, wiped out in the Jewellery Quarter bombings of December 1941; the grave is erected, a Christmas gift it says, by the grandmother, and one year later her name is also carved on the side. Dead, maybe, of a broken heart.

One night, they stand out in the back yard, watching the leaping red flames as Coventry is blitzed. You could see the fires, they say, as far as the channel.

I don't think they care too much when the war ends. "We were still too upset about Dad," says my mother.

My mother is happy at 2 Guildford St and at Cadbury's, and she is happy at the Youth Club, at Burlington Hall, at the Albert Hall. She is now very glamorous with her auburn hair, grey green eyes and peachy skin; "like a film star," people say admiringly. Her figure is perfect, and after she has given her wages to Nan, she is given pocket money to buy herself beautiful clothes from the Lozells Rd and the Co-op. She loves to drink and dance; she takes up archery, and she goes on camping holidays with the Youth Club. She has many admirers, and then she meets the one.

2. Dad and His Family

When he dies, Dad leaves us some six folders of family history. It has been his hobby ever since he retired.

It was difficult for him to trace his ancestors; we come from generations of labourers, whether agricultural or industrial, and the further back you go, the less information there is.

"Nobody bothered to write down the history of the working classes," he says sadly.

He does manage to glean information from old baptismal, marriage and death records held in Birmingham's oldest churches. Many of his ancestors have cause of death as 'exhaustion' on their certificates – worn out by agricultural or industrial labour.

Our name, he says, is an Anglo Saxon one, and he does look like an Anglo Saxon with his fair hair, bright blue eyes and high colouring. He does find a record of a William Holte being christened in St Martin's in the Bullring in 1500 – it's a name that crops up again and again in his family – and it's nice to think of a long line of blue eyed William Holtes through the ages from 1500 to the birth of my father in 1928.

Holte, he says, means a heath, yet he and all his brothers, his father, his uncles, all his known male relatives bear the names of royal dukes, kings and princes: William, Albert, Charles, Henry, John, Ernest; my father says with a nod and a wink that we are the true and dispossessed owners of Aston Hall, Birmingham's great stately home, or that we are the true descendants of King Harold, killed at the Battle of Hastings.

Birmingham, says my dad, is Warwickshire and that is Shakespeare's county, so we are even better than Liverpool and Manchester, Birmingham's perpetual rivals to be the Second City. But, he says, if we unite we can rule the world! Three mighty industrial cities, the workshops of the world, the cities of a thousand and one trades!

Dad's father is Charles Henry, a small man like most of his family, their height dragged down by the malnutrition that plagues the working classes. Confusingly, my father has two grandfathers called William and two grandmothers called Florence. The working class name pool is a small one, although rather curiously in my dad's family history there is a swathe of lovely classical names: Penelope, Cassandra, Irene, Diana and Sophia, and you think, where did they get them?

Charles Henry is born in 1894; he joins up in 1914, luckily for us in the Navy not the trenches, or we might not be here now. He survives the war, although he is at the Battle of Jutland and in 1919 he marries my grandmother, Letitia.

I have one photo of each of them. My grandfather gazes out from a photo in his World War One uniform. My grandmother Letitia peers out from the back of a wedding group, smartly dressed in a cloche hat and fashionable Twenties dress. The working classes always put on a big show at baptisms, weddings and funerals, the great festivals.

No-one has any memories of her, except her brother, my father's Uncle Arthur, who lives to be 100. "She was a good soul," he says. "She used to go with me to the dentist."

When she marries she has to give up work, as her life is taken up with childbearing. Like so many others, she and her husband live with his parents in a tiny terraced council house and you think, "How did they do it? What was their life like?"

Her first child, my Uncle Charlie, is born in 1920, followed by my dear Uncle Albert in 1921. Then there is a little girl, Joan Florence, born in 1924, but she dies in 1928, the year of my birth of my father Bill. Another girl follows in 1932, Jean Jessie, and a youngest son, John, in 1934.

My father has no memories of his mother, except one. She dies in 1937, of stomach cancer, shrieking in pain because the family cannot afford a doctor.

His father has always been a heavy drinker; now he becomes an alcoholic. He is a window cleaner – he has a round on the Witton Rd – he finishes at lunch time and drinks all his money away in the Holte Arms.

My father and his siblings fend for themselves. One of the things they do is pick up bits of coal dropped from the coal delivery vans; they go round houses trying to sell them. His father dies at last in 1939; there is a family legend that he died in the gutter outside the pub, but we don't know. The house is cleared out completely and everything thrown away; nothing survives of my father's childhood. We do not know what he looked like as a child.

My father is eleven. His elder brothers have joined the Navy to get three square meals a day, a wage and a decent uniform. My father is a very clever lad and he likes school. The school enter him for the eleven plus exam, so he can go to one of the great King Edward's Grammar Schools of Birmingham. He passes with flying colours, but he can't go. The three younger children have run wild after the death of their father; there is a short period in a Barnardo's home, then they are at last placed with various members of the family. My father ends up with his step-grandmother, now widowed; she is kind to him, but she has no money to buy him a grammar school uniform.

My father doesn't mind. He goes to the local secondary school. Then Birmingham is bombed; he comes home one lunch time to find half of his street gone.

"Half the children came home one day," he says, "and found they had no home and no family."

After that, he has a short period of evacuation, which he enjoys; the couple are kind to him and he likes the countryside. He is back in 1944, aged fourteen, and he starts work. He will work in factories for fifty years.

In the early years he drifts from job to job. There are plenty of jobs to be found in post-war Birmingham, as it rebuilds itself. On the other hand, there is a housing shortage – thousands of working-class terraces were destroyed – and he stays with his grandmother or sometime his friends. Much of his time is taken up with avoiding his National Service. As he doesn't actually have an official address or a permanent job, this is quite easy; he can just ignore his call up papers. Then the Forces begin to send people for him.

One day he is working at the depot at Aston Station, when one of his friends comes in.

"They're coming for you, mate!" he says; and indeed, a man in uniform is heading towards the station in quest of my father.

My father promptly hops on an incoming train; it takes him to the City Centre. He hops on a train for Leicester, and spends a pleasant day at the Oadby Races.

They catch up with him in the end; he wants to go in the Navy, like his father and brothers but there are no vacancies, so he chooses the Marines. His service doesn't interest him much; he learns to swim, which he likes and he goes to Malta, which he loves. On the day he leaves, his friend is just about to throw out a tin of photos he's taken of the two years; he's not interested, he wants to forget. But my father says, give them to me. These tiny black and white photos are the earliest pictures we have of him. He also buys his friend's camera, a Box Brownie; he will use that camera for the next twenty years.

He gets a job at the British Oxygen Company; he makes friends there who will be friends for life, Stan Atkins, Harold Styles, Roy McManus and Johnnie or Sean Bowman. He joins the Youth Club and goes to Burlington Hall; he plays football and darts and has all night card parties with his friends.

He has to travel sometimes all over Britain and he enjoys that. He goes to Liverpool, Birkenhead, and the Wirral a lot, fitting equipment into hospitals. He is in London when George VI dies and he stands with the crowds at the funeral.

"I saw four royal dukes," he says years afterwards. "Windsor, Edinburgh, Kent and Gloucester, walking in front of the coffin. I could have reached out and touched them."

3. Mom and Dad

My mother has many admirers, but she doesn't take any of them seriously. She is aware of my father in the background but she doesn't think much of his looks. People say the Holtes are plain with their long noses and big ears, but my mother doesn't like his fair colouring; she likes dark men, like her own family.

One night she walks home from the Albert Hall, up Witton Rd, to Six Ways, down Newtown Row, past the Orient and Globe Cinemas, turning right into Geach St, down to Guildford St, where she lives at 2 back of 37.

She glances behind her as she goes. She can see my father and it doesn't bother her – he lives around the corner – but he is walking slowly, hands in the pockets of his camelhair overcoat. She does think he is always well dressed. He always wears a suit and a dazzling white shirt and tie; his shoes are immaculately polished. The Marines have taught him that.

They meet, although they do not know it yet, outside 37 Guildford St, the house in which they will live with their young daughters for ten years.

They stand at the bottom of the entry – as it is always called – talking for an hour, but she can never remember what they talked about. He told me about his sad childhood, she says later, and that was enough; she's always been a sucker for a sob story. They talk for so long that my nan comes down, looking for Mom and she calls her in sharply. She has high standards of behaviour, even if she is a working-class cleaner living in a two bedroom council house.

At first, Mom won't take Dad home.

"He was so plain," she says later. "I was a bit ashamed."

But when they are dating seriously – or courting as it is called – Nan soon grows to like Dad. He gets on with all the family, as he usually does.

All their friends are coupling up now and they get engaged. Dad saves his money and goes to the Jewellery Quarter to buy a ring. Then they start saving for a wedding. It takes them two years – they don't of course have credit cards or overdrafts, just a paypacket every Friday. They put their names down for the council housing department, but the council can't rebuild all the houses bombed in the war fast enough so they're going to do what their parents did before them; live with a family member, Nan's dad, Grandad Hatfield, in Brook Vale Rd.

In the meantime, they enjoy themselves at the Youth Club, at dances, but most of all the cinema – the pictures. Musicals are their favourite: they take Uncle Bill to see *South Pacific*. Uncle Bill is a ballroom dancer, and a very talented one. He has a partner, Mavis, but he doesn't want to date her. Uncle Charlie has left school and is working in transport. Uncle John is still a schoolboy, enjoying playing cricket for Warwickshire Schoolboys. As for Auntie Eileen, she has done very well for herself. Both she and Charlie have inherited £100 each from their grandparents and she gets herself an office job, and takes classes in typing, shorthand and bookkeeping. She is going to become private secretary to Mr Wallace Lawler, the factory owner who is involved in various projects in the community; eventually becoming a Liberal Party City Councillor and then MP for Ladywood. It's said of him that he knows everyone and their problems, and he is the champion of the homeless and the underprivileged. It's because of him that Mom's family votes Liberal; Dad's family is Labour.

Mom's grandmothers both die in 1953 and she wants to put off her wedding, which is to be December 19th, but Nan won't let her.

"Your grandmothers wouldn't have wanted that," she says. Moreover, it has to be the 19th December as Uncle Billy is to give her away, and he will be on leave from his National Service.

Probably Nan is thinking that when Mom marries, she will very soon have a bedroom to herself as Auntie Eileen is marrying the year after. Charlie is courting Auntie Ann as well, and planning to move over to Bearwood, so she will only have Bill and John at home.

She doesn't approve of my mother's wedding dress at all. It's a beautiful white lace frock and Mom is having fittings for it, but she won't have a long dress. She wants ballerina length. Maybe she wants to show off her legs in white high heeled shoes. Her veil falls all the way down her back though, held in place by a wreath of white silk roses and she is having a huge bouquet of lilies and lilies of the valley – her flowers. As for Dad, he is not buying an off the peg from Burton's, his favourite shop. No, he is going all the way to Mr Hedley James, tailor's on the Dudley Rd to have his suit made, and he has been to Clark's and bought some daring suede shoes!

"They were in a sale, though," says my mother. "I just hoped on our wedding day that he remembered to take the sales sticker off. They were ten and six."

Uncle Bill is to give Mom away. He too has a new suit and shoes and my grandmother treats herself to a new coat and hat, which she can wear afterwards. The working classes would never dream of not buying new clothes for a wedding.

Mom is paying for the bridesmaids' frocks too. She has three: Aunty Eileen, my father's sister Jean and her friend Sylvie.

Sylvie, she explains to me many years later, was the child of first cousins.

"She had a hunchback, you see, and that was why I chose her. Nobody else ever had her to be a bridesmaid."

She's right about that; Sylvie is never a bridesmaid again, never marries, and dies young.

It's an act of kindness by my mother and all three bridesmaids look very glamorous on the wedding photos in their lace frocks, caps and satin shoes, all wearing a string of pearls (paste of course), which Dad has bought for them. They all wear satin elbow length gloves, because of the cold; my mother keeps hers in a box for many years after, yellowing with mother of pearl buttons.

All the family are out in force on December 19th 1953. It's a winter wedding and my mother makes her stately progress down the entry to the waiting car. She is extremely nervous – Uncle Bill has already been down the entry and reported that the whole of Guildford St is waiting to see her go.

My mother proceeds down the entry on Uncle Bill's arm. An admiring crowd awaits her. She looks like Ava Gardner or Linda Darnell. She turns her head left and right and makes a sweeping gesture with her bouquet as she ascends royally into the hire car. It is her moment.

The wedding, like all that of the family, is at St George's Church; if it wasn't here, it would be at Aston Parish Church. All the family baptisms, weddings and funerals take place at those churches and you'd never dream of getting married in the Registry Office.

"People would have thought that you were pregnant and had to get married," says my mother ominously.

The reception is at the Birmingham Co-op, another great institution of Birmingham, and after the reception they get on the bus to go home with Grandad Hatfield and that's all the honeymoon they have.

4. Wanted, a Good Home

Both my parents are now working full time; my dad wants to get out of BOC, because he doesn't want to travel anymore. Mom is doing well at Cadbury's. Neither of them want children; they've been part of large families all their lives, and they've had enough of that. Besides, in the days before maternity leave it would be a terrible blow to lose Mom's wage. But for some reason, they don't get a place of their own; they must be way down the Council housing list. They share their home with Grandad Hatfield and they're never alone.

Then, in 1956 disaster strikes. Grandad Hatfield dies. He is the official tenant of the house and the City Council tells them they can't stay there; it's a two bedroom house and it's going to be allocated to a family. As a childless couple, they are way down the list. They are sent to live in a hostel for young couples in Handsworth. Then disaster strikes a second time; my mother discovers that despite all their efforts to the contrary, she is pregnant.

My mother does what she can. She goes to Eileen and she writes to Mr Wallace Lawler. Mr Lawler is chair of an emergency accommodation bureau set up to find housing for the homeless; it was set up after a conference chaired by the Bishop of Birmingham. In bombed out Birmingham, people are living with their parents, in sheds, in air raid shelters. She can't have a baby in a hostel, but all Mr Lawler can find for her is a top floor flat in a high rise block in Northfield. Northfield! It's like the dark side of the moon and a two bus journey ride from Ladywood, and Dad will have to take the train to Birmingham city centre and then ride his bike to work in Perry Barr every day.

They accept it – it's all they can do – and move in. Mom has to give up her job at six months and they have to manage on Dad's wages. That's why he rides his bike to work; it saves money.

Dad has got himself a new job. He can't be doing any more travelling now, and one of his best friends has just been sent to Ghana with BOC!

He goes to Northfield Library to read the *Birmingham Evening Mail*, and he sees an advert for fitters at George Tucker Eyelets, in Perry Barr. It's an old established family firm, founded by George Tucker, the inventor of the pop rivet. The building is a beautiful art deco 1930s redbrick on the Walsall Rd. He writes to them and they write back; he goes to the call box and arranges an interview and starts there the Monday after. He sits on his bench and makes pop rivets all day; a clever man tossed out of school at the age of fourteen. What does he think about, as he sits at his bench all day? But he does make a friend for life, a genial Irishman called Johnnie Murray.

Tucker's, as he always calls it, does have the advantage of being close to Guildford St, a bike ride away down Walsall Rd to Six Ways and down Newtown Row. This is lucky, because four weeks before I am born, my mother moves back to my nan's. She can't be on her own in the flat, she states, so near her time; if she goes into labour, she has got to get down twelve flights of stairs and down the street to the public call box. So now Dad has to cycle from Northfield to Perry Barr every morning and clock in for 7.30 am; then at dinner time, he spends fifteen minutes cycling to Nan's, to see his wife. He has half an hour for dinner before he cycles back to work, and then at half past four he clocks off, cycles to Guildford St for his dinner and then cycles back to Northfield to an empty flat.

I time my entrance into the world well; on the 5th February 1957, he arrives at Nan's for his dinner at 12.15.

"Run down to the phone box!" she screams as he comes in. "Lil's gone into labour!"

Dad, she says later, stood there in his overalls, with his mouth open. He recovers in time to run down to the phone box at the end of the street and call for the ambulance; then he has to run back, grab his bike and a sandwich, and cycle off back to work. He can't go to the hospital; if he doesn't work, he doesn't get paid, simple as that.

I am born that evening, at 9 pm, at Dudley Rd Hospital. Nobody knows this till the next day, when my nan phones the hospital (again from the call box).

She and Dad and Uncle Bill catch the Outer Circle Bus to Dudley Rd that same evening (after Dad has finished work). He just has time to buy a few flowers on the way.

"And when I saw those flowers," says my mother who has had a shattering labour, "I could have hit him with them."

5. Name that Child

On the 6th February, 1957, Dad, Nan and Uncle Bill turn up at Mom's bedside. Mom is not very happy; she doesn't like the hospital, the food, or the nurses, she complains.

"Think yourself lucky," says Nan. "If it wasn't for Mr Bevan's Health Service, you'd have had to have that child at home. That happened to women in the nineteen twenties and thirties, and as like as not they or the child died. Your Aunty Min's baby boy died at birth, at home, and after that she had your cousins Gill and Hazel, and she always thought the baby would have lived if she had been in hospital." She falls silent, thinking of the baby girl she lost at home in 1940.

Mr Bevan is Nan's hero. She is indifferent to politics, thinking that politicians do not make the life of working class women like herself any better, but she makes an exception for Mr Bevan's Health Service.

"I go down on my knees and thank God for Mr Bevan and his Health Service, as I don't have to worry anymore about paying for the doctor, and I got my teeth done and a pair of free glasses!"

Attention now turns to me. I weigh a healthy eight pounds, and they are all very impressed with my thick, dark hair.

"The nurses fetched a hairbrush straight away and put a ribbon in it," says my mum proudly.

Apart from that, she is not too pleased. She expected a boy and she is not used to having her will crossed and no, she says, she hasn't thought of any girls names at all.

"I could call her Florence, after Floss," she suggests indifferently.

Dad and Uncle Billy look aghast. Floss herself hates her name, which doesn't have then the old fashioned charm it has now.

"I went to the pictures last night, and I saw this really beautiful actress," says Uncle Billy with enthusiasm. "The film was called *Trapeze*, and she was

Italian, and called Gina Lollasomething, but her figure!" He makes a gesture with his hands denoting an hourglass, and Dad laughs.

Dad says that his favourite actress is Marilyn Monroe, but he has just read in the paper that Grace Kelly, now Princess Grace, has given birth to a little girl called Caroline and he thinks that these are both really nice names.

"I think," says my nan firmly, "that if she's going to be named after an actress, it should be one who is a lady. Grace Kelly is a lady, and so will Princess Caroline be."

"Tuesday's child is full of grace," says Dad.

And so I get my name.

6. A Sister is Born

My mother has to stay, as you did then, for ten days in the hospital. She wants to go to 2 Guildford St when she leaves, but Nan is firm.

"It's not fair on the baby or Bill," she says.

My father hasn't missed a day off work during this time, as he'd lose pay. On the appointed day, he catches two buses from George Tucker's to Dudley Rd and picks my mother up. He has bought a carrycot to carry me in. Then they catch a bus into Birmingham and out again to Northfield.

Then the next day he goes off to work and my mother is alone with me.

She can't stand it; she is used to being with her family, or surrounded by work mates. She can't go back to Cadbury's as they can't afford childcare and my nan is still working. She's not the sociable type who can go to social groups and very soon she is depressed. Moreover, she is feuding with the neighbours; she says all the other women in the block of flats gossip about her and she screams at them from the balcony. She isn't the kind of lily that can be planted elsewhere; it's Lozells or nothing.

When the summer comes, she will catch two buses to Nan's in the evenings or at the weekend and my father is left in charge of me. He puts me in my pram and walks down to the local pub, The Man in the Moon; he orders a pint and sits outside the pub, placidly rocking the pram and sipping his pint. He has the gift of contentment.

Sometimes they will both go. I have a little pink pushchair which my doting Uncle Billy bought for me, and they put it on the bus and go over to Guildford St, and Nan and Uncle John walk with us to Aston Park or Tower St.

One day my mother puts on her very best jacket and skirt and dresses me in a fur bonnet and coat. She takes me all the way to Gerrard's Photography in Birmingham, and we have a studio photograph taken, both of us beaming at the camera. She is proud of her new haircut, with her Audrey Hepburn fringe, and a French beret perched on top of it.

But mainly she's depressed and she begins to nag Aunty Eileen; get onto Mr Wallace Lawler, get me a house in Aston. But she already lives in a two bedroom flat and she's just not priority.

Uncle Billy is now courting Margaret, who he will marry; she is Irish, blonde, a hairdresser and very glamorous. He takes her to see my mother in Northfield.

"She had the flat done beautifully but you could tell straightaway that she was unhappy," sighs my aunt many years later.

The unhappiness affects me; I am with her all day. I begin to cry for no reason.

Then disaster strikes for a second time. In January 1958, my mother becomes pregnant again. She is appalled; in the days before reliable contraception, all working-class women dread multiple pregnancies. Not for them the joys of the earth mother; it means losing your job, managing on one wage, bringing up children in two-bedroomed council houses with no hot running water or central heating, outside loos and no bathrooms. If you are lucky, you might get some 'piece work' to do at home, maybe making lampshades for Mr Wallace Lawler, but you don't sit around in a coffee shop with other yummy mummies rapping about motherhood and writing columns for *The Guardian*.

All through this second pregnancy, she is writing to Mr Lawler via Aunty Eileen; I can't manage here with two children, you have to get me back to Lozells!

Even Dad, normally so placid, is upset now; he thinks she might have some sort of breakdown.

Then she has a tremendous stroke of luck.

Guildford St is a street of back to back houses; my nan's house, no 2, is at the back of no 37, where an old lady called Florrie Price lives. She has brought up her two orphaned nieces there; one of the nieces has married and moved away, but the other, Gladys, still lives with her aunt.

Now Florrie dies and what happened to my parents happens to Gladys; she is not the rent payer and she has got to go, although she has lived there for over thirty years.

"I hope they find her somewhere," says my nan, but my mother isn't listening; she is already composing her letter to Mr Lawler.

My mother goes back into hospital on 21st October and my sister is born early on 22nd October 1958. My father takes me to see them both, but this time my mother's face is radiant; she is going home. She will never leave the hospital to go back to Northfield. My father brings with him the keys of 37 Guildford St.

It's up to Dad to arrange the move. In fact they have very little to move; he takes a deep breath and for the first time ever, now that he has a two-bedroom house to furnish, he buys some furniture on the Never Never. He goes to The House That Jack Built, the big department store on Newtown Row, and he orders some furniture.

The success of the move makes up to my mother the disappointment she feels at having a second girl. She expected a boy again and she has picked a boy's name: Leigh. She ignores my father's timid comment that he likes the name Susannah.

"It's as good for a girl as a boy and I'm not changing it," she announces. To make sure that no-one does change it, she goes off to the Registrar in Broad St on her own.

The Registrar's will is as strong as hers.

"I can't register a girl as Leigh," he says. "You'll have to think of another name."

But my mother stands firm and so does he, and after some discussion they reach a compromise. He will let her keep the name Leigh if the baby has an additional name which is uncompromisingly feminine.

My mother remembers, at last, my dad's preference.

"I'll have Susannah Leigh," she says sulkily.

Like me, she has a grand family christening at Aston Parish Church; all babies are christened into the church then, and she has the same godparents: Uncle Billy, Aunty Eileen and Great Aunt Floss. We are launched upon the world.

7. Home Sweet Home

I have written of my parents in the times before I knew them, from things that they told me; now I must write of them as I remember them. I have no early childhood memories, and so I must write from my earliest memory. I am standing in the door of the house, looking out on the street, and I am wondering what school will be like, and so my earliest memory is from 1961 as I begin school in September, when I am four.

As my sister is only three, my mother is still at home, and Dad is still working at George Tucker's.

I stand on the front step of our house in the summer of 1961, gazing into the street.

Our house is built in a bank of four back to back with my nan's. All the houses in the street are red brick terraced, dating from Victorian times. Someone has painted *God Bless Our Boys* on the front, which annoys me as it does not mention girls, but my dad explains it dates from World War One.

Our house, no 37, like Floss and Bert next to us at no 35, has a tiny front yard which most of the houses in the street do not: the front door opens straight onto the pavement. Not that there is much in the front yard. Two steps lead up to it and it is paved with concrete tiles. There is one large bush, planted by a long ago tenant. My mother has put a clematis against the wall, on a trellis supplied by my father; she will take that clematis when she moves and keep it all her life.

Nobody bothers to 'do up' their council houses, for which we pay the palatial sum of fifteen shillings a week to the rent collector. It's well known that the council could kick you out at any time, so what's the use?

Mr Ballenger, the rent collector, comes around every Friday with his black bag for the rent. He likes coming to our house as my mother offers him a cup of tea (he doesn't get so warm a welcome elsewhere). He doubles up being a rent collector with peddling Co-op insurance and my mother pays him her sixpence life insurance. So she won't have a pauper's funeral on the Co-op.

When we move in, Dad wallpapers and paints the house throughout, and has carpet laid, and that's it. It stays like that till 1968 when we leave.

Like all the houses on the street, it's a tall three-story house, and you walk in through the door straight into the living room, which has three doors: one which is always locked leading to the entry, one to the kitchen and one to the tall and winding stairs. There are two alcoves each side of the fireplace, into which my mother has fitted their twelve inch black and white TV and the radio. My father has built cupboards under them; one side for our toys and one for our books.

The living room is papered with yellow wallpaper decorated with chocolate brown roses. My parents have a suite, as they call it; a small green sofa and two matching armchairs. The sofa is situated under the bay window, so my sister and I can lean against the back, look out of the window with its net curtains and watch the world go by.

Everything is kept in the sideboard, a dignified piece of furniture on the wall opposite the sofa. It is dark brown, solid wood, kept polished to a high gleam by my mother. The four dining chairs are set against the wall, but the room is so small that there is no room for a dining table. We have a green baize card table which folds up. My father puts some nails on the wall, and it is hung up there. At meal times my mother takes it down, and puts on a gingham checked tablecloth. She sets it with *Cries of London* placemats, which we love, because of the pictures of pretty ladies selling oranges and lavender.

An oval mirror reflects the whole room, as it will reflect the family for sixty years; it hangs in my house today and sometimes when I look into it, I wish I could see that cosy room with its leaping flames (although my father is not so keen; he has to get up at 5.30 am to light the fire).

The kitchen is so small that once in it, you cannot turn around. It has a party wall inserted at a later date. Ranged across the far wall, which backs onto my grandmother's house, are the sink (cold water only), the gas stove, my mother's tiny twin tub (which she hates as it is very temperamental), and an array of wall cupboards and shelves knocked up by my father. The floor is really nothing but a trapdoor which leads down to the cellar which my mother uses as a larder, as it is so cool. My sister and I like to play there – my father has rigged up an electric light – and on Fridays we wait there while my mother opens the chained up grating and the coalman empties his sack into it.

The steep and winding stairs lead to my parent's bedroom on the first floor. My mother has a pale green carpet and pale green wallpaper as this is her favourite colour. The finest furniture of The House that Jack Built and the Co-op enhance their room; a double bed, two fine wardrobes and an entire dressing table suite, on which my mother keeps her jewellery box and brush and comb. She can sit on the matching stool and admire herself in the triple mirror. They have a three bar electric fire, as it is so cold when my father gets up and he doesn't want to have to be lighting two fires.

The next flight of stairs, getting even steeper and narrower, lead up to the attic, where my sister and I sleep. This room is even colder; it has a fireplace but my parents won't let us have a fire up here, there have been too many tragedies with fire on the street. So we can't get out of bed till we have put on our thick dressing gowns and slippers, and our pyjamas are thick winceyette. My mother has loaded the beds with blankets and candlewick counterpanes. We love our wallpaper, primrose with a selection of nursery rhyme characters, and we lie in bed making up stories about them.

My mother always has water on the boil on the stove, in kettles and saucepans; on Friday bathdays, there will be a bucket steaming there. My father will bring in the zinc bath tub, hanging on a nail in the backyard, and puts it in front of the fire; my mother erects a modest screen using her clothes horse, covered in towels. But me and my sister have to share a bath, which we think is very unfair; my parents have a bath each! But we do like our bath toys; I have a red and white plastic boat called Boaty, and she has a blue plastic duck called Ducky. We are not really into imaginative names.

Before the holidays, we go to the washing baths in Victoria Rd, where my father pays a shilling each for him and Mom, and sixpence for us. Then he goes off to the Men's side and we go with Mom into the Female Section. The baths are enormous, with claw feet holding them off the ground, and we can fill them up to the top with hot water out of a tap!

8. The Yard – our world

Floss and Bert live next to us in No 35, with our cousins Mark and David. They are separated from the Etkins by a passage, always known as The Entry, just as we are separated from the Luttrells at No 39 by The Entry. Up The Entry is the back yard, giving the Back to Backs their name; four houses backing on to us.

The Dockers back on to the Luttrells. People say they are Irish, but my father says no, they are Scottish, and their name should really be Deuchar. Mr Docker has a long, thin garden reaching out into the yard; we can peer through the tall hedge and see that he is growing vegetables.

On the opposite side is Mrs Minnie Owen, a very old lady, who always wears a flowery apron and carpet slippers; her grey hair is parted in the middle and drawn back into a bun. Her garden is the same size as the Dockers, but it is a tangled, overgrown wilderness. She likes to come out and watch us play; she stands with her arms folded, smiling at us, but we are frightened of her, she is so old.

The middle two houses belong to my nan and her neighbours, the Morrises. Jack and Ginny Morris have a dog, Bruce, which we are terrified of; it snaps and snarls at us, and is the cause of much conflict between the Morrises and my nan. The Morrises have a son, Dennis, but no-one ever sees him; away in the forces, says my dad.

Our Yard is a bit different from the other yards on the street and we are quite proud of it. The middle has a kind of heap of earth, like a playground, and exactly one half is covered with grass. We're not allowed to go on the grass as the Morrises say they planted it, and they'll set Bruce on us if we do. Working-class people are very territorial about property they don't actually *own*.

Two paths, one on each side, lead up to the top of the yard. They are bounded by overgrown hedges and to this day, I can see the white flowers of the privet, as I make my way up them. The top of the yard is a large, brick area where we play tennis, football and cricket with our cousins. It backs onto a large, red brick factory wall, empty now and derelict, but the men used to lean out of the windows and wave says my nan. Now if a ball goes through an open, broken window, we don't get it back.

What also makes our yard exceptional, in my view, is a collection of ramshackle buildings known as The Sheds. One is a lean to against the wall where my dad keeps his bike and our trikes. Another, in the centre of the yard, is made out of painted green wood and is known as The Little Green Shed, and my sister and I play there with Cherie from next door, when we aren't running round with David and Mark's Gang (of which we are honorary members). Next to this Uncle John's pigeon shed; Mom and Nan go in every day to feed his racing pigeons with corn and birdseed. Uncle John is only 13 years older than me, so he's more like a big brother.

There are four outdoor lavatories in the yard, in varying states, and again everyone, by some tribal rule, has their own; you never ever use anyone else's lavatory. I am glad of this, as they all look awful. My mom at least mops ours out every day and puts proper toilet paper, not newspaper, on a hook and Dad has whitewashed it; even so, I close my eyes tightly in there, as I am afraid of the daddy long legs and spiders that creep in. Moreover, Uncle John has a nasty habit of keeping little boxes of maggots in here for his fishing; my nan scolds him soundly for this.

The other shared building in the yard is the 'brewhouse' or 'brewus' as it's shortened to, where all the women of the back to backs do washing by hand. Again, there is an unwritten code as to which day you can use it; ours is Monday, and my mom and my nan would never show their faces there any other day. There is a big stone sink and a copper and a mangle. They have to boil the water on the stove in buckets and lug them up and wash everything by hand with big bars of green soap. Then they feed everything through the big box mangle, while my sister and I turn the handles. Then they pray for a dry day so they can set up washing lines in the yard, held up by big wooden poles. If it rains, there are wooden clothes horses in the houses, and my dad has rigged up two plastic racks attached to the ceilings; you put the wet washing on, pull on an arrangement of plastic ropes and up it goes. The smell of drying washing is overwhelming and then it's all got to be ironed on Tuesdays!

9. Nan

My nan sees me hovering at her gate.

"Come in for a glass of milk," she calls, and I run in joyfully (my mom says we must not "bother Nan because she is ill"). She had a heart operation in the 1950s.

My nan is nearly sixty and is looking forward to "Mr Lloyd George's pension". She exists on a war widow's pension and what she makes as a cleaner; her brother in law, our Great Uncle Jack, gets her cleaning jobs at the Law Courts, at Aston Library and Dudley Rd Hospital. She is five foot four and has never weighed more than six stone in her life. She is always beautifully dressed, in neat dresses with buttons and bows, or coats and skirts, and when she goes out, she puts on a lovely powder blue coat. Her heroine is the Queen Mother and so she always wears a flowery hat like the Queen Mother, and three rows of pearls and a brooch (except that Nan's are diamante and paste from Woolworths). Because she has had a lifetime of listening to BBC radio, she has a curiously 'posh' accent (also modelled on the Queen Mother). She has her hair set once a week at Marjorie's, Six Ways, and then she has to roll it up in curlers to keep. She ties a chiffon scarf over her rollers.

Nan always wears a flowery apron, or pinny as we call it. She now only has Uncle John and Uncle Bill at home, but Uncle Bill is engaged to be married, so soon she will have the middle floor bedroom, which she once shared with Mom and Aunty Eileen, to herself and Uncle John will have the top bedroom to himself. But we never go upstairs at Nan's. She has lived in this house since 1930. Like us, she has no indoor bathroom, no running hot water, no central heating. The furniture in her living room is sparse, but immaculately clean; a sofa and armchair, a table and two chairs.

You enter Nan's through the kitchen, which has a brick floor and a massive stone sink, but little else apart from a gas stove and rows and rows of shelves for pots and pans. It is always so cold in there that she doesn't need a fridge, and so the milk she pours me is freezing cold and she gives me a piece of a fruit cake she has baked herself, straight from the oven and piping hot. Nan has a cup of tea – the kettle is forever on the boil – she puts the hot water into a teapot full of tea leaves and when they get too weak, she just slings them onto the rather sickly plants growing in her small yard. She has a cigarette (everyone smokes) and reads, as she does every day, the *Birmingham Evening Mail* and the *Daily Mirror*, which she has delivered unless my dad can walk over to Cooper's newsagent on Newtown Row and fetch them.

What I like best in Nan's house is her radio and record player (which she has had since the 1930s, she has nothing new at all). They are made of Bakelite, and her radio has a curious wire front, with two plastic knobs on (on, off and sound). There are all sorts of fascinating foreign names painted on the grille, but as it is always tuned to the BBC Light Programme, it doesn't really matter.

I don't know why Nan has a record player, as she only has one record, Max Bygraves, singing a jolly little ditty about a mouse who lives in a windmill in old Amsterdam! All the same, my sister and I love this record. She lifts the wooden case; the record deck rests on green baize, puts on the record and drops the needle. The sound quality is awful, but we love it.

And so as my memory begins, the Sixties start, in 1961, as I go to school. I look at Mom and Dad and really see them for the first time.

Mom, like her mother, is always beautifully dressed, in dresses, or tops and skirts (she doesn't own any trousers) on a budget. She buys her clothes from the local shops, or the Co-op, except she always goes to Marks and Spencer or British Home Stores for her underwear. Like all the other women on the street, she runs a catalogue, and hers is Burlington, but she never buys clothes from there, because when they arrive they never look like the picture does. So I don't really know why she has one, but my sister and I like looking at the toys in there, and we love the Autumn/Winter edition, because it is full of photos of Christmas hampers.

My mother has all her favourite features, as though nature itself dare not defy her will. She has greenish-grey eyes and a peachy skin to which she applies make up every day. Her favourite lipstick is orange and her make up is Rimmel or Max Factor. She has reddish brown hair which she touches up with Rimmel, out of a bottle. Dad helps her touch it up every six weeks with the aid of two old toothbrushes and a plastic bowl. She sprays it with lacquer out of an Elnett Satin tin; the smell makes us cough but we love the picture of the lady with flowing locks. Then she also goes to Marjorie's on a Saturday morning to have her hair shampooed and set under a hairdryer. She tells Marjorie that she has heard of a new hairstyle, the 'beehive,' and she wants one done. Sometimes, if we need our hair done, she takes us, and we love sitting in the little hairdresser's, where the air is scented with setting lotion and cigarette smoke, and where the women gossip about everything under the sun; sometimes, they look at us and lower their voices. But mostly, they laugh.

My hair has lightened to brown and it's very fine and straight after a very short flirtation with curls. My mom has to wash our hair over a bowl at home with Silvikrin shampoo, and mine is terrible to comb afterwards. It's full of tangles and knots. Then Mom sees a picture in a newspaper of a young woman with a fringed bob, the geometric, or Vidal Sassoon cut they call it...

"We wore our hair like that in the Twenties," sniffs my nan, but Mom takes the picture in, and Marjorie gives me a Mary Quant haircut.

I don't like it I want long hair and I don't care if it is in plaits. My sister has a ponytail. No-one cares about having to make a fuss with her hair because it is a really beautiful mane of long blonde curls. Marjorie shampoos it, exclaiming over its beauty and gives it a really light trim. My mother ties it up in a ponytail with a big bow at the back of her head; if Floss is knitting bonnets for us, she leaves a hole for it to be threaded through. My mother has a huge collection of ribbons for my sister's hair and she keeps them all her life.

My mother dresses us alike, which we don't like much either, but she lets us have our favourite colours; pink for me and blue for my sister. We wear kilts and jumpers in the winter and dresses and cotton shorts in the summer, all bought locally and Floss knits us cardis and bonnets. She has a knitting machine, but she prefers to knit by hand and she never needs a knitting pattern; all her designs are out of her own head.

Like all of his family my dad is not a tall man, he is five foot seven. After being one of the thinnest marines ever to join up for National Service, he has put a bit of weight on thanks to three square meals a day and my mother's cooking. He still has bright blue eyes, a high colour and curly fair hair. He cycles off every day to Perry Barr in his blue overalls and a mac and peak cap in case it rains. My mother gives him some 'snap' in a lunch box, but really she wants him to come home for lunch, which he does; he's had enough of a transient lifestyle.

At weekends, like my uncles, he blossoms forth in immaculate shirts, trousers and jackets; people have always said he was a 'snappy' dresser, and like Billy and John, he polished his shoes and ours with Cherry Blossom, so you can see your face in them.

"It's because I was in the forces," he explains.

10. The Early Years

I don't really want to go to school, I enjoy being at home.

My mother thinks that when both of us are at school, she might get a job and then if Dad learns to drive, they could have a car. Bert can get one with an employee's discount from Rover. She can't get back to Cadbury's yet, it's too far, but she could walk to Lucas's, Great King St or Hampton Row, and get a job on night shift there, 5.30 – 8.30 pm, because that's what Floss has done now David and Mark are at school. In the meantime, she manages with her catalogue and piece work making lampshades at home from Mr Wallace Lawler's factory, and what Dad brings home in his pay packet on a Friday. Neither of them have a bank account and credit and debit cards are unknown, so they count out the money and put it into carefully labelled jars; Rent, Rates, Water, Gas, Electricity, TV Licence. Then they put some money into the Post Office on a Saturday morning for The Holidays. Whatever is left over, it's for food and the newspapers and the occasional cinema trip, and that's all there is. My parents can manage and they don't want anything to do with Social Services, or Parish Relief, it's a badge of shame, says my father, wincing as he remembers his *Daily Mail* boots.

My mother has never been on a six week parenting course or read any books on parenting skills. Her views are that she thinks children should be clean, well fed, well dressed and well behaved, and of course able to read and write, otherwise how can you get a job? Not that she knows what we want to be, but they are determined that we don't go into the factories and maybe, they think vaguely, we could work 'for the council'. White collar, not blue collar.

Mom doesn't take us to playgroups or mother or toddler groups; really, she is just too busy to sit around and chat with other moms. She wants us to join the Brownies and the Girls' Life Brigade when we are older, but that's different, we can stay there.

Our day begins when she wakes us up at 8 am. Dad gets up at 6 am and lights the fires and then pedals off to work. Breakfast is cornflakes and toast, although at the weekend we have bacon sandwiches on Saturdays, and a full English on Sundays; bacon, eggs, sausages and mushrooms. We have a weak cup of tea. Coffee is virtually unknown on the street, although my dad, who fancies he is a bit cosmopolitan because he was abroad for two years, has a little bottle marked Camp Coffee, with a soldier and turbanned Indian on the front, which we find very exotic. The milk is delivered by the milkman, who leaves us what we call a fat bottle and a thin bottle; one is sterilised, or stera, and the other pasteurised, or pas.

My mother expects us to eat everything put in front of us; she has no time for food fads and whatever the grown ups eat, we eat. Lunch is always a cheese sandwich between slices of white bread and butter, and it is butter, not margarine. Sometimes we have corned beef, which we really love and then you can put HP brown sauce on it. There is a HP sauce factory at Aston Cross, and when the wind blows, we can smell the sauce being made. Or we might have a boiled egg and 'soldiers' made up of Sunblest white bread with butter on (we never have margarine, it is a badge of shame). If we have had beef for dinner on Sunday, we might have a piece of bread with beef dripping thickly spread, from a jar where the jelly has gathered at the bottom, or we might have a 'lardy' sandwich sprinkled with salt and pepper. Another favourite is corned beef, straight from the tin with a little key, and with brown sauce.

My mother does not really approve of cakes, but she might give us a slice of Harvo loaf as we call it, with butter; or maybe at a weekend, a doughnut or a custard tart from the baker's. Lardy cake is another favourite with a crusted sugar topping and bread pudding with raisins.

Mom's morning is always taken up with shopping and we go along too, which we really like (but she doesn't). Then home to get Dad's lunch. In the afternoon, she puts our toys out for us. The house is so small that they are kept in a small cupboard under the TV, except for our dolls and teddy bears, in our bedroom. We have little prams and pushchairs to push our dolls around in when the weather is fine. We have board games like Snakes and Ladders, card games like Snap, a fine Jack in the Box, and jigsaws – my sister can do jigsaws when she is two. But the afternoon is learning time.

My mother has an abacus, a wooden frame with beads on it, from one to twenty, all painted in different colours and tasting delicious if you lick them. Patiently, and using her fingers also, she teaches us to count to twenty. I don't like this – it makes my head spin – but I do love it when she gets out her flash cards and teaches us the alphabet.

She waves them in front of us: A is for Apple! B is for Ball! C is for Cat! D is for Dog! We do love the pictures on this and she also has a rag book, bought from The House That Jack Built, with the alphabet in it. She has a nursery rhyme book which she reads to us and we sing along with her.

Up till 1961 we only have a radio and we listen to *Listen with Mother,* which would no doubt be today *Listen with Parent/Carer.* My mother is a devotee of the BBC Light Service; she *never* listens to the Home Service or the Third Programme as they are la-di-da. Her life revolves around a relationship with the DJ; at the end of her life she will listen to Chris Evans and Jeremy Vine as happily as she once listened to Jimmy Young or Terry Wogan.

In 1961 my parents purchase a 12 inch black and white TV and my sister and I discover the delights of *Watch with Mother.* We love watching the flower opening at the beginning and we see *Picture Book* on Mondays, *Andy Pandy* on Tuesdays, *Flower Pot Men* on Wednesdays, *Rag, Tag and Bobtail* on Thursdays, and *Tales of the Riverbank* on Fridays. I like *Picture Book* best, and I wish I could read. My dad laughs at *The Woodentops* and says they exploit Mrs Scrubbitt; he is always saying things like this since he became a shop steward and the Union paid for him to go on courses.

Many years later I will revisit these programmes through the miracle of DVD, and the flickering black and white images and the poignancy of the music will reduce me to tears as few things can do. Why did I never realise that they were so sad?

Dad gets home at five, cycling down from Perry Barr, just in time for a good brown dinner, as my nan calls it. Mom always makes stew on Mondays with leftovers from the weekend, lots of vegetables and pearl barley, and dumplings which we love. Tuesday is pork chops, Wednesday sausages and Thursday veal. Friday is Dad's pools night and so he brings us fish and chips on his way home from the Greek's as everyone calls the fish and chips shop, whether they are Greek or not. Saturday is a piece of pork and crackling, and Sunday is a full roast beef and Yorkshire pudding, with gravy, and a pudding afterwards. I like rice pudding and sago or semolina, especially with a bit of strawberry jam in it, but mainly we have apple and blackcurrant crumble or apple pie, with Bird's custard.

In the week, we are sent to bed at 7 pm – Mom and Dad want some time alone – but on Saturday, we are allowed to stay up; we curl up on the sofa with them and watch TV.

On Sunday night we can watch *Sunday Night at the London Palladium*, but sometimes my parents will have the radio on for a bit of easy listening, and they do like the Shipping News.

"We have to think of the sailors out at sea," says my mom, but for some reason I want to cry when it is on.

11. Retail Therapy

The milk is delivered every day by the Co-op dairy; it saves my mother having to carry it and of course, like everyone on the street we don't have a fridge. The cellar doubles up for that. My mother washes out the milk bottles and leaves them, gleaming, on the step. The milkman also delivers potatoes and bread, eggs and orange juice and cheese; anything, really.

The postman calls three times a day, there are three deliveries and they say if you post a letter to someone in Birmingham in the morning, they will get it by tea time. The post man wears a smart navy blue uniform and a peaked cap. We love it when it is our birthdays and he knocks on the door with a handful of cards and maybe some parcels; one birthday, aunty Eileen sends me an exciting parcel all wrapped up in brown paper and it is a jack in the box!

Coal is delivered too on a weekly basis and when my sister and I are at home, we help. We lever open the grating outside the front window, set into the front yard, and we watch out for the coalmen. We like to see them in their aprons and gorblimey hats; they are, quite literally, black as coal.

They empty the sack of black gold down the grate, and we go down into the cellar to check it has all arrived safely. Everyone has coal fires, and the smoke from the chimneys and the factories combine with the fog in Autumn to form the dreaded smog, swirling yellow and grey and so thick that you need a torch to see. My mother ties scarves over our mouths when we go out in it, but we still cough.

Another home visit is the chimney sweep and we help with that too. He is a small man, bent double, with two front teeth missing, so he whistles when he talks and of course, he is as black as soot. But the cloths he drapes over all the furniture are immaculately white. He fits his brushes together and sends us outside, walking down Geach Street, till we can see the brush poke out of the top of the chimney, and when we rush back, there is soot everywhere!

Our other callers are the gypsies, as they are called. My mother and nan do like to buy their wooden pegs. One day my mum is up at Nan's and two gypsy lads come to the door. They have two puppies and ask me and my sister whether we want to buy them. The lads have soft voices and queer accents; we are entranced by the squirming puppies till my mother returns, and that's the end of that.

My mum and nan feel sorry for the tinkers, as everyone calls them. They drive their caravans onto patches of waste land, and stay there till the police evict them. Sometimes, as the gypsies leave, the council workmen put piles of earth up round the waste ground, and the little children make half hearted attempts to push them down.

No-one on the street drives, so whatever services call are welcome. The rag and bone man comes round to take away anything you don't want. Brought up in the war, my mum and nan are extremely thrifty; make, mend, sew, patch, sides to middle, so we don't see him so often, but my sister and I like to listen for his mournful cry, "Rag and bo-oo-one!" so we can rush out and see his horse and cart, and offer the horse an apple or maybe sugar.

Another home delivery is Dad's Davenport, which arrives in a crate. It does last a bit, because he only has one on a Saturday night when he is watching *Match of the Day*. My mother is annoyed that my sister and I can sing along with the jolly little Davenport's TV ad, where the bottle bounces from one word to another, but my father laughs and says it is teaching us to read.

My mother buys our clothes on the Lozells Rd, and sometimes the Co-op. She takes us for shoes to Clark's; we like sitting on a stool and having our feet measured on the scales.

Our family has always been well dressed, on a budget, but suddenly, everyone is becoming well dressed. The girls on our street are all sporting beehives or geometric cuts, and some of them are wearing mini skirts! They wear them with high heeled court shoes – white is popular – or maybe boots, also with a high heel. As for the lads, they are all sporting sharp suits and ties and high heeled boots on their feet – Cuban heels or Chelsea boots – the influence of The Beatles, or so they say, and Cathy McGowan on *Ready, Steady, Go*. They all look so glamorous as they pass down the street on Friday nights on their way to a hop at the Albert or Burlington Hall, or up Geach St on Saturday night, to get the bus into Birmingham.

My mother and nan always go to Marks and Spencer's or Lewis's in Birmingham, though, for underwear. It is the mark of a True Lady. If they want a winter coat, they might splash out and go to Grey's, the big department store in Birmingham City Centre.

As we do not have a fridge – no-one has a fridge – my mother shops every day. There is a small shop on our street – Rudhall's, or as everyone calls it, Ruddles – my nan will send me down there for her cigarettes and I like to look at all the chocolates and sweets in the window, in big glass jars. If we have a penny, we can have some measured into a small white paper bag, or we can buy a jubbly in a cone of plastic paper and when the jubbly melts you can drink the juice! We like all the chocolate bars too, laid out in such tempting array; if I have some pennies, I always choose the Picnic bar. My sister likes the Bar Six, but we also like to look at the tasty array: Kit Kats, Mars Bars, Caramac and Maltesers. "Buy Cadbury's!"

Newspapers and comics come from Cooper's Newsagents on Newtown Row. My mom goes there every day for her shop, or maybe Summer Lane. There is every kind of shop you can think of and best of all a Woolworth's, where my nan buys us our very first purses and little handbags. Mine is purple and my sister's is orange; we open and close them so many times that the clasp soon goes and we have to fasten them with an elastic, which isn't the same.

We like the butcher's, with his shining brass scales and the baker's, with the smell of freshly baked bread and cakes, although my mother is not a great one for sweets and cakes. We have three square meals a day, supper, and all the fruit we want, so what else is needed? But I do like the doughnuts with their choice of three fillings, jam, cream or custard.

There is a market on Newtown Row where my mother goes for fish, which we don't like as they lie mournfully gazing at us with their dead fishy eyes. But she only buys kippers here for a weekend breakfast. We do always have fish on a Friday, but it's breaded and produced by Captain Birdseye.

On Fridays Mom and Nan toddle off to the Lozells Rd, and do a Really Big Shop for the weekend, with their wheeled shopping trolleys; they come back exhausted and panting. We do like going there with them if we can, as there is a pet shop where they have kittens and puppies in the window. There is a china shop where my nan buys her Royal Albert Old Country Roses, and when we have pocket money, we buy Mom something for Mother's Day, maybe a pickle jar or a milk jug.

My father doesn't like shops – he only ever goes to Burton's the Tailor's – although he does go to White's Ironmongery on Summer Lane for his tools.

On Saturdays Mom catches No 5 or No 7 into Birmingham City Centre. She doesn't take us – we stay at home with Dad, listening to the football results on the radio – this is her time. She likes the Bull Ring Market, and Marks and Spencer's. She always brings us a present back; I remember little baskets made out of plastic, red for me and yellow for my sister.

She only takes us in the holidays and reluctantly, because of the bus fare, and as it is so crowded. But we love going up and down the escalators in Lewis's and Rackham's, which we have to do because toys are right at the top. We love Barnaby's Toys in the Great Western Arcade, and Hudson's Bookshop and the Midland Education Company and WH Smith's book department. And then we love catching the bus back from the bottom of New St at six o'clock, as the pigeons wheel and caw overhead in the darkening sky.

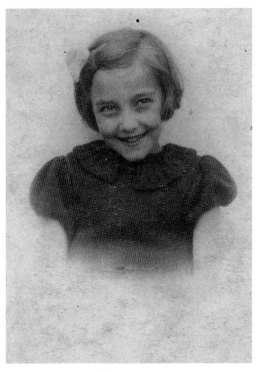

Mom, 1937.

On the beach at Paignton, 1959.

At Bigbury Court Farm, 1960s.

The author in 1957.
Studio Portrait by Jerome.

Bridesmaids at Uncle John's Wedding, 1964. Front row, left and right.

Mom, 1948.

Out walking in Northfield, 1957.

Dad and his car, 1962.

National Service, 1950. Dad middle row, 5th from left.

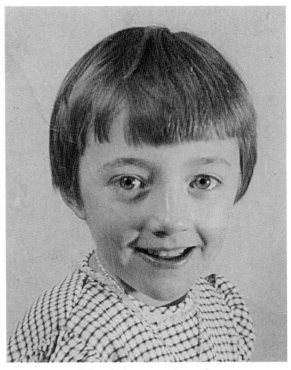

Floss and Bert on their Wedding Day.

School photograph, 1964.

Author and sister in Guildford Street, 1959.

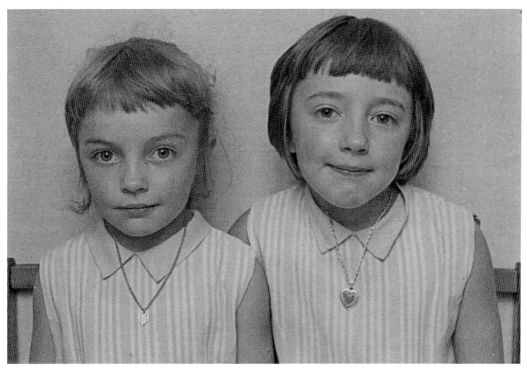

School photograph, 1966.

Mom and Dad's Engagement photo, 1951.

New Year's Eve charabanc outing. Mom and Dad on the right.

Burlington Hall Youth Club Football Team, 1950s. Dad on back row, second from right.

Nan in 1939.

Mom and the car, 1963.

Mom dancing at Burlington Hall Youth Club with Barbara Atkins, 1946.

The street from our garden, 1960.

Day out at the Lickey Hills, 1965.

Easter Holiday at the caravan, Porthmadog, 1967.

12. Unwillingly to School

Birmingham has two intakes for school; September and January, but as I am four in February 1961 I will start school in September 1961.

I want to go to my mother's school, Lozells County Primary it's a few streets away, but she has told me so much about it. I only last there a week; the school is too far away and too big, and I come home in tears on one Friday.

My mother is a woman of action. She writes a note to Lozells, to say I am not coming back, puts a first class stamp on and sticks it in the post (they will get it Monday). Then on Monday, she marches me, my sister in tow, up Geach St, to William Cowper Church of England Infant and Junior School. They accept me immediately – they need the numbers, no-one wants the old Victorian church schools, they want the new county schools – and I embark on my state education.

William Cowper is situated on Cowper St, and it was originally Cowper St School; they changed the name to make it sound more posh. The Infants occupies half of the building and Juniors the other. I am to be with Miss Cope and the Infants for two years, till I am seven.

Miss Cope is a big lady with carefully set iron grey hair. She wears an A line dress and black court shoes, and looks a bit like Agatha Christie. There are only two classes in Infants, with Miss Reid and Miss Reeve, both older ladies with silver hair, who wear a blue overall. I can't remember much about the infants. We have an assembly every morning, where we chirp *All Things Bright and Beautiful*. We have a morning break with chocolate marshmallows and a little bottle of milk, but I can't drink the milk, it's not like the milk I have at home. All the same, we still have to sing:

Thank you for the world so sweet!
Thank you for the food we eat
Thank you for the birds that sing
Thank you Lord for everything!

Then, when we have finished, we carefully fold up the blue check table-cloths, shaking out the crumbs and put them away. I am also a flower monitor – I change the water in the jam jars and vases with flowers on the teacher's table.

I like water play and sand play, but best of all, I like the reading books we are given, the *Wide Range Readers* which are full of exciting stories. The teachers are a bit put out by the fact that I can already read.

In 1964, I start the Juniors, as my sister begins the Infants.

William Cowper is a big old Victorian building, erected to serve the poorest children in Birmingham (which we are not, but we live very close to it). It is also a Church of England school, so we have Assembly with hymns and prayers every day. We have to learn the hymns line by line, with Mrs Burton, who plays the piano.

It is a two storey building, with a bell tower and very high ceilinged classrooms, surrounding a central hall with a polished wooden floor which doubles up as the dining room. The lavatories are just off it, where you wash yourself with scratchy carbolic soap, and there are also some in the small playground, which we avoid, because of the spiders.

Every classroom has single rows of wooden desks and chairs, with the teacher sitting at the front, next to the bookcase set in the wall, and the blackboard, as they are still called. A blackboard and chalk are all the teachers have to teach us the three R's. We write with sticks of wood set with a wooden nib, which you dip into the inkpot set into the desk. It is someone's job, the Ink Monitor, to fill these up every day from a huge blue bottle. The Flower Monitor waters the flowers on the teacher's desk, or whatever we are growing on the window sill (usually broad beans on blotting paper or coleus flowers) and the Door Monitor opens the door when the teacher comes in.

Every child who passes into the Juniors has a reading test with Mr Sims, the headmaster who has replaced Mr Powell. Mr Sims is tall and thin, wears a black suit and tie, and has his hair plastered down to his head with Brylcreem. His office is on the first floor, next to that of Mrs Wardell, the school secretary.

The reading test consists of reading single words on a sheet of paper on Mr Sims's desk, in ascending order of difficulty; the list starts with *a, the, and, but*, and progresses down the page. Mr Sims holds a blank piece of paper over the lines, and moves it down as you progress.

Well this is easy, I think, as the paper slips further and further down, and soon I am reading the last line: orchestra, applaud, concert, conductor (is there some sort of theme here?) As I finish, I look up and see Mr Sims staring at me.

"Well, little Grace Holte," he says with a shake of his head, "I can see we can't teach *you* much about reading."

He frowns, takes his pen, writes something on the form in front of him, then Mrs Wardell pops her head in the door, and asks him to come and check the dinner money. Mrs Wardell is a cheerful soul, with immaculately set red hair; she wears nice flowery dresses and court heel shoes.

As soon as he is out, I sidle up to the desk, to see what he has written in red pen:

Grace Holte. Age 7. Reading age 14 years. Really Excellent.

I am one of those children who is picked out to be 'groomed' for the eleven plus; that is, I will miss the bottom class and spend two years in Top Class, attending extra classes on past papers.

There are only 50 children in the school altogether and there are 5 years; Top Class, Class 2, Class 3, Class 4 and Class 5 (which I am to miss). A legacy of Mr Powell, most of the teachers are Welsh and they speak Welsh in the staffroom, which you hear when you are a Tea Monitor and you go to the staffroom to make tea for them (and cough on their cigarette smoke).

The teachers are Mr Ellis, Big Mr Jones, Little Mr Jones (who is over 6 foot but younger), Mr Webb (whose class I miss), Miss Jones (later (Mrs Francis), Mrs Burton and Mr Tapper, who always teaches Top Class.

The only other teacher is gentle Mrs James, who comes in on a Tuesday afternoon to teach the girls needlework, while the boys go off for crafts. She is very old, with immaculate white snowy hair. She tells us that she was born in James St in Swansea, which we think is funny, as it is her name. She shows us how to thread a needle, how to do simple knitting, how to crochet, and how to embroider our names and the dates of our birth on a square piece of cambric with holes picked into it.

The school day hardly varies from year to year, and we enjoy the settled routine. We are a church school, so we begin every day with Assembly in the Hall. Every class marches down the stairs and takes their seat on the highly polished floor; we don't have chairs. The Hall soars all the way up to the arched roof of the school with its bell tower which is no longer used. It also doubles up as the PE room, so we are surrounded by apparatus. Mrs Burton sits at the front at the piano, playing a march as we come in and Mr Sims presides over us. Behind him is a board with four ladders, showing four little men, red, blue, yellow and green climbing up ladders. These are the school houses, and we call them by their colours, but Mr Sims says they are really St George, St Patrick, St David and St Andrew. I am in Yellow House, which is nice because it is St David, and the teachers love St David's Day because he is Welsh like them; we always get the rather sad story of Gelert on St David's Day, and we sing *Men of Harlech*. You get points for your house by being a monitor or doing well at Sports Day, and the big trophy is awarded at the end of each year.

We always begin by singing; the school that sings together stays together. Then we have prayers and Mr Sims tells us a story from the bible, and then we have notices. Sometimes we have a bit of entertainment; some of the children will recite, or the recorder group plays songs.

On Fridays the Reverend George Brown comes in from St George's. We enjoy this because he brings his guitar and sings with us:
Dance, dance whoever you may be!
I am the Lord of the Dance says he!
Kum by ya my Lord kum by ya!

We also get nice little sermons on being good (this is a church school) so generally we are in quite a quiet mood when we march back to the classrooms.

Monday morning is *Singing Together* with the BBC, and it's a nice way to start a dismal Monday morning. Every classroom has a very large radio with a huge speaker, and the book monitor gives out the BBC *Singing Together* booklets. We have a new one every term, with a pretty cover which I like very much. The voice of Uncle William Appleby leads us as we pipe together:
Now I was born a poacher lads, in famous Lincolnshire!
Pack up your troubles in your old kit bag and smile, boys, smile!
Lilliburlero, hey now now!

The Beeb, in a conscious effort at early multiculturalism, includes songs from Wales, Ireland and Scotland, so we also trill:
Men of Harlech, bound for glory!
It's a long way to Tipperary!

There is obviously a Jacobite at the Beeb (my dad says it is Lord Reith, as he is a Scot), because we sing loads of songs about Bonnie Prince Charlie:
Bonnie Charlie's noo awa! Will ye no come back again?
Come o'er the stream Charlie, dear Charlie, brave Charlie!
Speed bonnie boat like a bird on the wing, over the sea to Skye!

At the end of each term, we all vote for our three favourite songs and there is a special edition in which Uncle William announces the winners and we sing them for the last time. Thousands of children across the nation trill their favourite songs at the same time. We are Singing Together.

Wednesday mornings is PE although we don't have much apparatus in the hall; a climbing frame, a wooden horse and some benches, so we spend a lot of time doing keep fit. As with Playing Fields we have to use the shorts and tops provided by the school; the tops are knitted and orange and the shorts blue. They have been through many a generation of children and I don't like them because I think they smell. I find a plain knitted top and try and pick it out every week.

We wear black pumps, slip-on or lace for PE, and I don't like these either, as you can never find a pair that fit. But some of the children just keep on the ones they are wearing already. Some of the children do not have shoes; they wear pumps all year round and in the winter, they don't have coats, just cardis and jumpers with holes in.

I don't realise that some of the children are very poor till an incident at school. My mother always gives me a chocolate Penguin biscuit to eat at morning break as we don't get the marshmallows anymore that the infants get, although we do get a quarter pint of milk and orange juice, neither of which I like. The school does sell biscuits in one of the classrooms, and you might be selected to be on break duty, although the older children are supposed to do this as it helps them with their number skills for the eleven plus.

At twelve o'clock, the hall becomes the dining room. Tables and chairs are wheeled out by the caretaker, and the dinner ladies come in with their huge covered tins of food and you can smell it through the whole school. Lots of the children get free school dinners, and some of them have school dinners because they live some way away but their mums work at Spartan Steel just opposite the school and it's handy.

But I go home for dinner, with my dad, who has driven down from Tucker's and my mother and sister. We have dinner at lunchtime because of my mum going off to work in the evening as soon as Dad gets home. My appetite has always been a bit dodgy, so my mother is very surprised when suddenly I start eating all of my dinner.

"I was so hungry," I say one day, emptying my plate.

Instantly suspicious, my mother questions me. Under interrogation, and almost in tears, because somehow *it is all my fault,* I admit that I put my

Penguin in my desk every morning before Assembly, but by break time it is *gone*.

My mother, to my horror, accompanies me back to school that afternoon and insists on seeing Mr Sims who launches an immediate investigation. The culprit is caught and punished, but to my mother's horror, it turns out to be poor Malcolm, one of the poorest boys in the school, who has holes in his trousers.

"If I'd have known," says my mother, shaking her head, "I'd have bought him one of his own."

Thursday is playing fields day. The big Birmingham City Council double decker bus rolls up outside the school, and we all fight to go upstairs and sit at the front. The playing fields we think are a bit boring, all flat, not like the park, and really all we do is the boys play football or cricket, and the girls play rounders and in winter it is *freezing*. Sometimes we prepare for Sports Day, so we practice the sack race, the egg and spoon race, the wheelbarrow race, the obstacle race and the flowerpot race.

Friday is music with Mrs Burton. Every class has their set time to march down into the hall and stand before the old upright piano, which Mrs Burton plays so beautifully. She tells us that she has won prizes for playing the piano at something called the Eistedfodd.

We don't have songsheets, so our way of learning songs is to repeat a line and sing the line till we know it; then we do the same with line two all the way to the end of the song. Over fifty years later I can remember every song I sang at school:

Yellow bird, up high in banana tree!
Michael row the boat ashore, alleluia!

A particular favourite is a ditty called *Westering Home*, which my sister also learns (every child, every year, learns the same songs). My father asks us to trill it to him later, when we have the car, and he thinks we need entertaining during long journeys.

We also learn all the hymns for assembly, as we don't have hymn books. Mrs Burton plays a line and we sing it; then she adds another and we sing two, till we can sing every verse of every hymn. *Gentle Jesus, meek and mild,* we pipe, a hymn a day, but Easter and Christmas are much more exciting.

Friday is also folk dance day – the teachers are winding down a bit – we have taped music for this in the hall and we take our partners for the Morris dance.

Sometimes in music we have percussion instruments; tambourines, sticks with bells on, triangles to be tapped with a little stick and xylophones which we love. I am also a member of the recorder group, because my parents think it's a good idea. The school has a set of wooden Adler recorders, but I enjoy this so much that my mother goes to Yardley's music shop on Snow Hill and buys me my very own recorder, in clear white wood and Floss makes me a little blue case for it. But I am too shy to play in Assembly.

We have morning and afternoon playtime, and we have to go out whatever the weather after we have had our council milk and marshmallows. Some of the children shiver in their little cardis and pumps, but I always have a winter coat, hat, scarf and gloves. The boys play football, which we like, as it stops them turning their attention to us and playing a game called Kisschase. The only way we can escape them is by leaping onto the railings, and yelling "Acky acky acky!"

We girls play skipping rhymes, with a huge long rope:
Spanish lady, turn around! Spanish lady, touch the ground!
Spanish lady, do the kicks! Spanish lady do the splits!

Or:
I'm a little girl guide dressed in blue!
These are the actions I must do!
Bow to the king
Curtsey to the queen
And twist right round to the fairy queen!

There are some rude versions of these songs involving showing your knickers, but they don't sing them when the teacher is around.

Other games sweep the playground; sometimes we join hands and circle under each other, to form a ring, singing:
Oh the big ship sails on the alley alley O, on the last day of September!
Sometimes the girls will put a small rubber ball into an old stocking, and stand back to the wall, stretching their arms and legs as they bounce it into the empty spaces. Or we form a ring and dance ring a ring o'roses, until the school hand bell, rung eight times a day, summons us to class.

Two of the girls get a length of elastic and stretch it over their ankles to form a square. They sing:
All in together girls!
This fine weather girls!

When I call your birthday
You must jump IN!
January! February! And so on ...

I jump right in on February, and you have to keep one foot in and one foot
out and hop, but by December, there is a real scrum.

"Such *silly* games," sniffs Mrs Burton disapprovingly.

We have Parents' Evening every term, where we do displays of dance and
song, and our parents have the chance to look at our work and admire our
handicrafts. In the summer term, we have Sports Day, but my parents can't
come, they are working. The other special day at school is an annual visit from
a travelling theatre company. They put posters up all around the school, and
my parents give us the shilling apiece we need to go.

On the appointed day, the theatre company set up a little stage in the hall;
we hang over the balcony watching. After dinner, we are marched down class
by class to the hall, chattering with excitement. Some of the children have
parents who can't afford to pay, but Mr Sims lets them hang over the balcony
and watch. The theatre company acts traditional tales such as Sleeping Beauty
and Aladdin and for me it's the beginning of a lifelong love of the theatre.

Of course, as well as the school choir and recorder group, we also do plays.
In the Infants, I was in the Nativity play, but my mother was very cross that I
was only an angel and not the Virgin Mary. So she ignores the instructions
given out to equip your angel with a silver tinsel halo. I am the only angel
with a golden tinsel halo.

We perform *Snow White and the Seven Dwarfs* twice in junior school (why
waste a good script) and in the first production I am Bashful the Dwarf, with
a little wheelbarrow.

"It's because you are so shy," says Mrs Burton; she is reading us an exciting
book called *Rikki Tikki Tavi*, and she calls me her little mongoose, because
she says I enter a room like the mongoose; I creep in around the corners
instead of crossing it. Maybe to compensate, the next time round she gives
me the role of Snow White and I get to wear a pretty dress for a change. The
year after I am the Sleeping Beauty, but apart from my tall pointed cap made
out of paper, with a sweeping gauze veil, I don't like this because Philip, as
the Handsome Prince, has to kiss me awake and all the boys snigger.

The school day, apart from the above, is reading, writing and arithmetic.
We don't do history, geography or science and of course we don't have to do

computers. Every assembly is followed by ten a day spelling test (which I love) and a recitation of the times tables (which I hate). We learn the tables off by heart and I don't understand them, but as my mother says, why bother to understand them? Just *learn* them.

In a complete disregard of Health and Safety laws, we stand on our chairs as we go round the class chanting the tables, and if you get your five times five is twenty-five times wrong, then you stay standing. So you might as well learn your tables as it's a mark of shame to be last one standing.

Spelling is easy, but if we get a word wrong, we write it out five times till we know it.

Reading is done with the *Wide Range Readers*, and every level is a different colour. I read mine straightaway, I love the stories so much, so it's a good thing there is always a shelf of books in each classroom, kept in a rolldown cupboard, and the school library, which is a classroom with some lock up wooden cases. We also have silent reading and the teachers reading aloud to us, so we are really fluent readers.

Once a month a man called Mr Spence comes in with something called the Reading Lab. Mr Spence has thick glasses and unkempt hair and we think he is very funny to look at, like Ken Dodd. There are ten levels on the Reading Lab, graded in order of difficulty and each has a colour: Orange Lab, Purple Lab and so on. You read a little coloured booklet on a topic, like canals in Venice and then you answer questions. My sister and I enjoy this so much that we create our very own Reading Lab at home with paper, crayons, sticky tape and an old shoe box. It's just like the comic *Look and Learn* Mom gets us, which is kept in a neat folder, and which I often re-read apart from the week about dinosaurs which I think is a bit frightening.

Writing is done with a little nib attached to a wooden pen and you dip it in your inkwell. But one year we are given blue biros and the inkwells become obsolete. Mrs Burton says with a sniff that our writing deteriorates as well. But I do love writing stories in my little lined writing book.

I really do hate sums, for which we have small grey notebooks with squared paper in. Addition, subtraction, division and multiplication are all obstacles over which I have to leap, and as for fractions and decimals! My mother and father have no sympathy with this; they can do sums in their heads, but the teachers shake their heads, as I have got to pass a mathematics paper for the eleven plus.

I only like sums when we are allowed to use wooden blocks in a box, ranging from twenty tiny white little squares all up to one big red wooden block. We put them together: three green blocks plus two yellow blocks is five blue blocks.

We also have Topic Afternoon, which I always think sounds like a chocolate bar. We have to choose a subject and write about it every week in our little grey note books; we use the books in the school library or the classroom to do this. The trouble is that all the girls want to do Nature and all the boys want to do Football. I like doing Costume, as I can look at history books with lovely pictures of historical clothes in. I especially like the Georgian ladies with their big powdered wigs.

If you are lucky, you might get chosen to be a monitor. During my time at school, I am a Flower Monitor, an Ink Monitor, a Door Monitor (opening the door for the teacher) and best of all a Tea Monitor. You can leave lessons to go to the staff room, where you switch on the urn, put the cups and saucers and spoons out and arrange Lincoln biscuits on a plate. You cough all the time you do this, as the teachers smoke so much that there is always a miasma of smoke in the room.

And so the school day passes peacefully, punctuated by the ringing of the brass school bell (lucky pupils are chosen for this duty), till it is four o'clock and home time.

13. Friends and Teachers

I make a friend in the infants called Chrissie and I love her. Chrissie is one of those children who only wears cardis and pumps, and her cardi has holes in. She lives with her mother and a swarm of siblings, in one of the terraced houses in the maze of small streets around Cowper St.

You know, says my mother many years later, that her mother was a prostitute?

No, I say, I didn't know that, how would I know that?

She has left by the time I go into the Juniors, the family moved to one of the houses in the new council estates at the edge of the city. I miss her very much.

Really, I like the boys best. Philip is a little gentleman and my mother approves of him very much and I also like fair haired Alan and dark haired Ronnie, and serious David. My best friend is Sandra, tall with dark curly hair. Philip and Sandra actually come from Erdington, but their mums work in Spartan Steel opposite the school, so it's much handier for them to come in and go home on the bus with their mums because there aren't any breakfast or after school clubs. If it comes to childcare you are on your own, and all the mums work. Sometimes Sandra doesn't want to be my friend and she goes off with Karen who is tall and sassy, and then I turn to Veronica or Linda Broadfield or Tina or gentle Helen who minds her little sister so well. Helen comes from a very poor Irish family and should be at the Catholic school, but my mother says that her mother doesn't care. She gets upset about Helen's ragged clothes. Helen, she says, is a *good* person.

You have to have a best friend; it is a mark of shame not to.

The teachers aren't interested in what kind of background we come from. As far as they are concerned, we are there to learn how to read and write and hopefully pass the eleven plus and get to grammar school or if not, be well equipped for an apprenticeship or clerkship. That's the way that most of them came up; from mining families in Wales who got them to teacher training college, and that's the best way to escape the poverty trap.

All the teachers have very distinctive personalities.

Mr Ellis, my first teacher, is tall and thin. We have an aquarium in his classroom and one year I proudly bring a huge sea shell which I have picked up on my holidays and he puts it straight into the aquarium which really upsets me. I wanted to keep my shell and put it to my ear and hear the sounds of the sea.

Old Mr Jones, who is not really old, is a short, chubby Welshman who rides a motorbike and we love to see him roll up every morning in his leathers and helmet. He has a soft voice and is very artistic. He takes art and encourages all to paint with our jam jars of water and our tins of paints and tiny brushes, or to draw with our Caran d'Ache crayons.

Young Mr Jones, who is young, is tall and handsome, but he has a very fiery temper and I am quite frightened of him.

Miss Jones, who becomes Mrs Francis, is small and pretty, with short dark hair in a Mary Quant cut and very fashionable mini skirts and dresses, which the boys love, especially when she turns around and reaches up to write something on the board with chalk (a board and chalk are the *only* teaching aides our classrooms are equipped with).

Some of the older girls wear mini skirts too, but my sister and I are stuck in cotton dresses and kilts, as my mother thinks it is "not suitable" for little girls. Miss Jones has a pretty, lilting Welsh accent and it is a joy when she reads aloud to us, which she does a lot. She reads from a book called *The Lion, the Witch and the Wardrobe*, and she breaks off at an exciting point each day, so we can hardly wait for the next instalment. I ask her the author's name, C S Lewis she tells me, and so off I go to the library to get all his books out.

She encourages me to write my own stories. When I leave her class, she gives me a book, a paperback all about girls who ride horses and have exciting adventures, and they live by the sea.

"It's because I enjoyed your stories so much," she explains.

The next class is Mrs Burton's, which we have all been dreading, as she is famous for her sharp tongue. She is a thin Welshwoman with horn rimmed glasses and carefully set red hair, and she plays the piano beautifully. I feel sick on the morning in September 1965 when I get up to go to her class for the first time, and I keep hoping that it's a mistake. But the first morning in her class is very peaceful, and soon I *love* Mrs Burton. Like Miss Jones, she encourages me to read and write and I take my own books into school to show her. Her favourite exclamation is "Ye gods and little fishes!" which makes us laugh.

Mrs Burton's outstanding talent is for playing the piano and singing, and so every year it is a small group from her class who are selected to sing in the Birmingham Junior Schools' Choir concert at the Town Hall. Top Class can't do it as they are busy preparing for the Eleven Plus.

A small group of six is hand picked. In truth, none of us are good singers, as Mrs Burton is the first to point out, but we are clean, well dressed and well behaved and have parents who can be counted on to turn up at the concert.

Mrs Burton tells us the story of the Manchester Schools' Children's Choir who made a famous recording of *Nymphs and Shepherds* back in 1929.

"Of course, none of you are as good as that," she reflects, but whatever Manchester (or Liverpool) does, then Birmingham must do also.

The school is sent a sheet with twelve songs printed on it; Mrs Wardell slaves over the massive Xerox machine to get copies run off for us, with smudgy ink.

"You have got to learn these off *by heart*," warns Mrs Burton, handing them out.

None of them are songs I know – one has a very melancholy chorus: *Apple, apple falling on the water, By the Stream I kissed the miller's daughter* – which is embarrassing for us girls. Another starts cheerfully:

Give to me the life I love!
Let the lave go by me!

We have just mastered the music when it changes in the third verse:

Or let Autumn fall on me!
Where afield I linger!
Silencing the bird on tree!
Biting the blue finger!

Every Friday we stay in the hall after Assembly and to Mrs Burton's accompaniment and conducting, warble the songs, which we don't actually like as much as the ones she teaches us.

The day arrives when we are to go to the Town Hall and meet all the other children, and the conductor and the City of Birmingham Symphony Orchestra. This is quite an adventure as we are going to get the No 5 bus down Summer Lane to Birmingham Town Hall. Mrs Burton is quite cross as the first two buses just sail past the request stop.

"They just don't want to take the children," she says angrily, but despite this we do get to the Town Hall early, and we have time to look at the pretty fountain which plays in the square.

We all have to file into some very high seats; Mrs Burton whispers that it is where the City of Birmingham Choir sing. We are fascinated by the Orchestra, who have musical instruments the likes of which we have never seen before.

The conductor is a very tall, thin man dressed in a grey suit and he carries a baton. He is not too impressed with our singing and he writes to all the Heads of School complaining; Mr Sims reads the letter out in Assembly and we and Mrs Burton are fit to die of shame. Despite this, we enjoy our bus trips and our rehearsals and the concert takes place in the end on a beautiful spring evening. My parents are dressed up to the nines; my father has his suit and tie, and my mother her bronze silk dress and beaded belt under her astrakhan coat. She makes sure I am well dressed too.

The Town Hall is a blaze of beautiful flowers when we troop in to take our seats; the hall smells of lilies and roses. I can't see my parents in the audience, only a sea of faces, but we sing our hearts out and the audience stands up to us. After, I meet my parents in the square outside; it is still light, and the fountain is playing and the pigeons are calling overhead.

14. My own private Library

I have been able to read since my mother taught me the alphabet. She doesn't have trendy ideas on education, or read books written by experts. She uses alphabet blocks and books and an abacus for counting, at which my sister is very good.

My father does his bit too. I like to sit on his lap at night as he reads his *Daily Mirror*; he runs his fingers over the words, explaining how the letters form a word, and the words form sentences. H A R O L D W I L S O N spells Harold Wilson!

In this way, I discover the exciting adventures of Garth and laugh at Andy Capp. From an early age, I am reading columns written by Keith Waterhouse and Willis Hall, and I especially enjoy Kingsley Amis' poetry column.

My sister and I enjoy the Live Letters, conducted by the Old Codgers, and we like it so much that we devise our own newspaper, the *Soppy Times*, held together in the corner by a piece of wool.

It's rather curious that my mother, who has not read a book since she was fourteen, encourages us to read so much. She thinks reading is a skill you just have to learn like your numbers; but she is puzzled that we actually *enjoy* reading.

"Still, with her head in a book, she's no trouble," she sighs.

Every week, she brings us an exciting roll of comics from the newsagent's Cooper's on the Newtown Row. My sister only likes the *Dandy* and the *Beano*, but I have a mass: *Diana, Bunty, Mandy, June and School Friend* and *Judy*. I lose myself in a fantasy world reading these comics. Girls at boarding school having midnight feasts! Girls learning ballet and dancing at Covent Garden despite all the machinations of their rivals! Girls who buy a broken down old pony and end up jumping for gold in the Olympics!

David and Mark loan us their *Eagle* and *Hotspur*, so that we can follow the exciting adventures of *Roy of the Rovers*.

We can't have too many books as we have no storage space, but my mother does buy me books from The House that Jack Built: a book of nursery rhymes, a book of bible stories and a picture book of Sleeping Beauty who has a lovely pink dress. My nan buys me books from the second hand shops, mainly Victorian children's books. The words are hard, but I struggle through them.

When I am older, my mother thinks I should read the classics, really because they are the only books she has heard of. The House that Jack Built sells children's books published with names like Blackie's Children's Classics or Collins Children's Classics, and so I get to read *Black Beauty, Kidnapped, Treasure Island, Alice in Wonderland* and *Little Women,* which is a particular favourite. As the books are not abridged, the print is very small and so I widen my vocabulary and develop bad eyesight, or so my mother thinks. There is a family legend that I read *Ivanhoe* at the age of four it's not true, but I certainly do read *Jane Eyre* (unabridged) at the age of seven.

Certain books, like certain films, are banned because they reduce me and my sister to tears: *Black Beauty, Greyfriars Bobby* and *Lassie Come Home* fall into this category. Anything about animals, really.

My mother has heard somewhere that every civilised house should have a Bible and some Shakespeare. Accordingly she buys a second hand Bible from the SPCK shop in Birmingham. The language is too hard for me although I like the sound of it, but we love the maps of the ancient world in the back.

She can't quite run to Shakespeare, but I do get a *Tales from Shakespeare* by Charles and Mary Lamb. Some of the stories are too sad for me, but I love the comedies like a *Midsummer Night's Dream* and I admire the pretty names of the heroines.

Warwickshire Lads and Lasses, we sing at school and Dad says we were born in Warwickshire, just like Shakespeare, or Warks as it appears on the post.

"Girls", says the headmistress of my grammar school, many years later when Birmingham has ceased to be in Warwickshire, "girls, you must always remember that you were *born* in Warwickshire, because it is Shakespeare's county."

At school, we have a small library in each classroom and the school library, such as it is, is enclosed in a couple of lock up cases, but I read the same books over and over. I especially love *The Wind in the Willows*, so much that my mother finds me my own copy; I come home from school one day, and there it is, on the pouffe next to the fireplace! I borrow a book called *Tales of the Greek Heroes* so much that Mr Sims eventually gives it to me. I have it to this day.

When I am five and my sister is four, my father announces that he is taking us to join the public library. He takes us to Birchfield Library in Perry Barr, not Aston (we don't know why) but we love it, the long corridor leading down to the library with the Reference Library and the Reading Room off it, and the smell, maybe of the book binding, and the coolness of the air. We have three blue tickets and we can borrow three books for a month each.

Birchfield is rather sophisticated in having a small children's library situated behind the issue desk; my father can dump us here while he goes off to choose his Alistair MacLean thrillers, so maybe that's why he chose it.

We love the children's library, the first books I borrow are the *Little Grey Rabbit Series*; I read my way through all of them. I also love the colourful Topsy and Tim books, and I try and read the Monday book on Monday and the Tuesday book on Tuesday, but as we only go once a month, this doesn't always work out.

Then I progress to books about ballet, boarding school and ponies, which seem to be my favourites, and very soon I have favourite authors, which helps me to find out how books are kept order. The lives of the girls in the books I read seem so different to mine, but I'm not jealous, I'm enchanted by them.

It never strikes me that none of the books I read are set on council estates or in state schools, nor do I care. My sister is reading a book called *The Family from One End Street,* which seems to be a family more like ours, but my father laughs at it.

"How the other half think the working classes live," he says to my mother; he is always talking like this since he became a shop steward and joined the Labour Party.

I love fairy stories as well, and after looking at them some time (they seem so formidable in their old fashioned red binding), I discover the works of E. Nesbit and Elizabeth Goudge. Really I don't mind how a book looks, and many of them have been re-bound in spotted binding to extend their shelf life, but I don't turn my nose up at them, I like the smell.

"The child could work in a library," says my mother hopefully. "She's always got her nose in a book."

15. We're all going on a Summer Holiday

My parents never went on holiday with their families, and my nan has only ever been to Blackpool on a day trip.

Until the nineteen forties, my parents are members of the Burlington Hall Youth Club. This is run by Bob Slack and his wife, who are both Quakers (for whom my mother has a soft spot), and they arrange camping holidays mainly down to Devon. Everyone travels down in a huge coach, and they have the time of their life; no-one has ever seen the sea before, but my mother's fondest memories range around the discovery of scrumpy. She also buys herself some daring new clothes for these holidays: shorts and slacks!

My father travels the world during his two years' national service; it gives him a love of the sea, even though like Nelson he is seasick.

When my sister and I are two and a half and one year old respectively, my parents decide that we are *going on holiday*. This of course means during the Factory Fortnight in July, which is just after the schools close for the summer holiday, and they set up a special Post Office Savings Account, so they can save up for a whole year.

In the days before the Internet and the mobile phone, booking a holiday means buying the *Evening Mail,* and reading the adverts for caravans. My father finds a holiday camp called Sun Valley in Paignton which sounds just right, because there is a train from Birmingham to Paignton.

On Saturday morning, with a pocketful of change, he goes to the public phone box on the corner, and makes a call to Sun Valley and books us a caravan in July for a whole week.

He then runs up to the Post Office on the Lozells Rd, and draws out a postal order, made payable to Sun Valley; this goes off in the Saturday morning post with a letter in his beautiful copperplate handwriting. He will pay the balance on arrival.

Now my mother is busy, sorting out clothes and toiletries to keep us for a week in Devon. She uses the savings to buy us all new clothes: short sleeved shirts for my father, pretty sun frocks for herself and for me and my sister, shorts and cotton frocks, and sandals and lace up pumps. She is determined that we are going to be the best dressed family in Sun Valley.

My sister and I are especially thrilled with the purchase of sun bonnets. We have two each: a cotton one with a turn up brim, red for me and blue for my sister, but much more exciting are straw sun hats with fringed edges and strings to hold them around our necks. My mother doesn't have one; she just buys herself some silk head squares, knotted under the chin rather in the style of the Queen. But she has bought herself some very glamorous high heeled white sandals with a peep toe.

As we are travelling by train, all of this plus towels has to be packed into my father's battered old travelling trunk which he bought from someone while he was in the Marines. It is covered with all sorts of exciting destinations, but we do hope our luggage doesn't end up in Malta. My father has bought some sturdy labels from the Post Office and my mother addresses them carefully to Sun Valley, tying them on with string.

British Rail come to pick up the trunk the day before we go – my dad has already been to Snow Hill Station to pay for this – and my mother has a stricken look on her face as she waves it off, rather as if she is saying goodbye to her own child.

On the Thursday night we catch a bus to the washing baths in Nechells, armed with towels, shampoo and bars of soap. My father goes off to the Gents when we arrive, leaving my mother with us in the Ladies. It's a beautiful red brick Victorian building and the baths themselves seem Victorian; very tall, with claw feet and shiny gold taps.

My sister and I can hardly believe that you can have so much hot water straight from a tap! My mother has bought some bath salts, little sweet smelling pink cubes, Boots Old English Lavender and she carefully breaks them up and adds them to the foaming water. Our hair is given a good wash too, with Silvikrin, but we don't need to go home with dripping hair, because there are long tubular hair dryers attached to the walls.

On the Friday that we are due to leave, my father is at work as usual, but arrives home for this two week break in tearing high spirits. He has already been to New St and bought the tickets, and now he goes to bed for a couple of hours to get a rest as we are travelling on the overnight train. My mother and my sister and I have already had afternoon naps, and my sister and I are dressed in our shirts and shorts, ready for travelling.

My mother has packed two bags for travelling with sandwiches in, but we can't carry too much as there is my sister's pushchair as well. In fact, it's easier to walk to Snow Hill than to catch the no 5 or 7 down Summer Lane, as the conductor might be a bit grumpy, so at ten o'clock we walk up the dark entry to say goodbye to Nan, who has never been on a holiday apart from a day out in Blackpool on a coach. She is sitting at the table, smoking Peter Stuysevants, drinking a cup of tea and reading the *Evening Mail*, and she gives me and my sister a sixpence each to spend.

It is still light as we set off down Summer Lane to Snow Hill, passing all the brightly lit pubs (and there are a *lot*). My father says drink is the curse of the working classes. My parents encourage me to walk as they really don't want to carry me as well as two bags and my sister's pushchair, so I trot along holding their hands.

Snow Hill is heaving everyone is waiting to catch the night train like us. Everyone is going to Paignton, Weston super Mare, or Rhyl. There is nowhere to sit down, so my mother holds me up to see the big steam train as it comes in, but I am more interested in grabbing her earrings, which are pearls surrounded by diamante, worn with her astrakhan coat with a fur collar, her flouncy summer frock, high heel peep toe sandals and a silk headsquare over her freshly set hair. My mother is going on holiday in style. As for my father, he is wearing a sports jacket and lightweight trousers over a short sleeved shirt, and he carries his mac over his arm.

There is a scramble to get seats – of course, no-one can afford a sleeper – we are lucky to get seats by a window in a carriage, my mother on one side with my sister and I on each side of her, and my dad right opposite. He falls asleep straight away and so do my sister and I, heads drooping onto our mother.

Bearing a load of snoozing Brummies, the great train pulls in at Paignton in the early hours of the morning. "Too early for anything!" says my father brightly after his nap, but my mother, who hasn't slept at all, looks crushed, literally and mentally. My father finds a space for her to nap on a bench, while he takes me and my sister on a walk round the station, but it doesn't last long because at nine o'clock we can walk down onto Paignton High Street for breakfast. There are two places you can have breakfast; The Hamby Bar and the Polar Milk Bar, but my father prefers the Hamby Bar where we have a fry up and weak tea in thick white cups.

By this time it is ten o'clock and we can at last check into Sun Valley Holiday Park. My mother has been worrying all night about the trunk, but it is there in Reception, and a porter staggers down to our caravan with it. My father pays the balance owing, with a wad of notes, and we get the keys to our caravan. Our caravan has cold running water, but not much else – for baths and toilets we need to go to an outdoor shower block, but we do that at home anyway so we don't care. The first thing my mother has to do after unpacking is make a list for shopping; we can't eat out every meal, she says. After paying the bill, my father has £27 for the next two weeks.

My sister and I cannot remember these early holidays too well, but we do enjoy them, despite the fact that I have to walk everywhere (my parents are too exhausted to carry me and they need to save on bus fares). The day always starts with a fried breakfast, usually fried bread and baked beans, or maybe sausages and bacon. Then my mother makes cheese and tomato sandwiches to take down to the beach, which we can walk to and fills up the big thermos flask with tea for her and Dad. We do get a bottle of pop each and a promise of an ice cream on the beach.

On the beach, my dad rents a couple of deckchairs for Mom and himself, puts on a straw hat, and announces with a stern air that as he works hard all year round, he expects to *enjoy* his holiday. This is aimed at me and my sister.

Through a complex arrangement of bath towels, we are all able to change into beach wear; matching swimsuits for me and my sister, and a very glamorous black one piece for my mother. My father is happy with his old blue swimming trunks which date from his time in the Marines.

Our time on the beach is spent playing with the buckets and spades which my mother buys us from a beach shop, but after his nap and his sandwich lunch, Dad takes me and my sister down for a paddle. We love the sea – we have never seen anything like it. Birmingham doesn't even have a decent sized river. My mother sits in her deckchair writing dozens of postcards, as we won't see anyone for two weeks and nobody has a phone so we can't call them. My nan gets two postcards, one to say when we've arrived, and one to say when we'll be back. She treats us to a candy floss, pink and sticky, or maybe an ice cream with a flake or an ice lolly. My mother likes a Cornish Mivvy, a red ice lolly with cream in the middle and Dad loves a choc ice.

Paignton Beach is very long and sandy, and faces a row of colourful hotels painted in all different colours, and we all pick a favourite building. Mine is pink of course and my sister's yellow. We can walk right up into town for dinner, usually at The Hamby Bar, although my sister and I like to go the Milk

Bar where we can get a milk shake, which is a real treat. I like strawberry and she likes chocolate. They take us to the pier, where my sister and I love the magic mirrors which distort our shape, and we use our pennies in the slot shows, where you can put in a penny and see Dracula arise from his tomb, or a skeleton dance. My dad has a pocketful of pennies for the shove halfpenny, but he likes the one-armed bandits and the horse racing games. There are four horses racing to win, so we can pick one each and the jockeys all wear different colours!

Then it's back to the caravan for an early night. My parents can't afford to go out and drink, and they can't take us into the pub anyway. One night, they do take us for a walk on the cliff tops for the thrilling sight of a storm far out at sea.

It does seem, looking back, that the sun always shone on these holidays, but it can't have done. Time flies too quickly till it's time to pack the trunk up on the Friday of the week after, and get it up to Reception for British Rail to pick up, and we have to manage with hand luggage for the walk back to the station Saturday morning and the long trip home.

One holiday when I am four, and about to go to school, my parents are walking around Paignton with us when they stop to look at a small car in a showroom window. It is £450.

"If I learnt to drive and we got a car, it would be much easier to go on holiday," says my father.

"When Susie goes to school, I'm going night shift at Lucas's," says my mother. "Then we can put all the money in the post office and save up."

And this is what happens in 1962. My mother would in fact like to go back to Cadbury's but it is too far for her to travel in the evening. She might go back there when we go to grammar school. So she does what Floss has already done, she walks up to Lucas's Great Hampton Row, and asks for a job on the evening shift. She is accepted immediately, Monday to Thursday 5.30 – 8.30 pm.

Now my mother has to get all the cooking and shopping in the day, plus the school walk six times, to be ready to go out at five o'clock to walk to work. My father leaves work at half past four and cycles straight home. We have already been washed and dressed in our pyjamas and had our tea and his is waiting on the table. As he comes in, my mother goes out, like the two figures on the musical box Uncle Bill brought her from Germany when he did his National Service.

Always a good worker, my mother is soon promoted to supervisor on her line, and this means more money. The Union also train her up to be Shop

Steward, and send her off on training courses about Health and Safety. She has a boss called Mr Laker who we are always hearing about; poor Mr Laker spends much of his time barricaded in his office while my mother lectures him on employment law.

We hear so much about Mr Laker that in our eyes he is some kind of ogre. We only meet him once. Lucas's have a Christmas party every year, and my mother is an aunty. You aren't supposed to have your own children in your group, but my mother takes no notice of that. So she becomes our aunty as well as our mom.

Very glamorous in her black beaded dress, beehive and orange lipstick, she is escorting our little group to the canteen for sandwiches, jellies and ices, when a little man materialises in front of us, rubbing his hands together in an ingratiating way.

"Oh Lily, please do introduce me to your lovely little girls," he says insinuatingly.

My mother draws herself up to her full height on her black court heels.

"In front of my girls, I'm Mrs Holte to you, Mr Laker," she hisses, and the little man collapses like a burst balloon.

My mother's steady progress coincides with my father's promotion to chargehand at Tucker Fasteners and to celebrate he buys himself two white shirts wrapped in cellophane. He too is a shop steward, and the union pay for all his training.

My parents, who don't miss a day in fifty years, aren't in fact terribly interested in what they do. Work is just something where you turn up every day and do your job and it pays the rent and the bills, and you can save up for the holidays. But now my dad has a savings account for a car and he is learning to drive on a Saturday morning.

My mother picks her pay packet up on a Friday morning and Dad gets his Friday afternoon. On Friday night he also picks up the commission from his pools round.

He comes back from this laden with fish and chips which we are allowed to eat straight from the newspaper and after my mom brews up a huge pot of tea while they pool their wages. Out come the jam jars, carefully labelled: Rent (with the book in it), Water, Gas, Electric, Rates. My mother puts her Co-op life insurance half crown in another jar for Mr Ballenger to collect when he comes for the rent (you don't want a pauper's funeral). My mother gets the family allowance for food and she also puts a half crown aside to go into her post office account.

"It's for school uniform for you," she explains. "If you pass the Eleven Plus and got the grammar school, you need the money for uniform. Your dad passed and he couldn't go because they couldn't afford the uniform. It could have made a big difference to his life."

Dad puts ten and six aside and everything that is left over goes up to the Post Office on the Lozells Rd on Saturday morning for The Holidays and The Car.

As he can only afford one lesson a week, it takes him two years and several attempts to pass his test. On his third go, Nan and Uncle Bill come down from the back and wait for us.

"He's been gone such a long time that he must have passed," says Uncle Bill hopefully; as he is a lorry driver, his firm paid for him to take his test.

Indeed, when my father gets back he is beaming all over his face; he has passed on his third attempt. My mother puts the kettle on and my nan passes around Peter Stuyvesants, and Floss and Bert come in from next door to join in the fun.

"I can get you a discount on an Austin," says Bert, who works there. This means a huge difference, so next Saturday Dad goes up to the post office and draws out enough for an Austin A40 and puts it into a little suitcase which Bert carries into Austin Longbridge.

Dad's car arrives the Saturday after, driven by a worker who will get the bus home; he leaps out and shakes hands with Dad, who takes proud possession.

"Wait, wait," shrieks my mother, "I'll take a photograph," and she runs for the old Box Brownie and crosses to the other side of the street. There he stands, a proud young man, hand on the door of his very own car, the door open as my sister and I peep out and it is all his own work. It is the first car on the street and all the neighbours are on their doorsteps. It is a great thing on the street!

Now we can go on holiday and my nan can come as well, sitting up in the back of the car between us, but every silver lining has its cloud, as my parents soon discover. I am travel sick. I am sick when I get in the car, I am sick when it moves off, I am sick most of the way. My parents try everything – feeding me, starving me, opening the windows, giving me Junior aspro. Nothing works. Even Dr Carolan is at a loss.

"We'll just have to take lots of carrier bags," says my father, deeply annoyed as he has to listen to me retching most of the way.

He has found a bed and breakfast in the newspaper and written off with a postal order deposit. Now all we have to do is pack the trunk and put it on the roof in a special luggage rack: Uncles Bill and John help us do this. As they do, Uncle Bill tells me that when he gets married, they are planning to go to Spain for their holidays. I am deeply impressed. Apart from National Service, no-one in the family has ever been abroad.

We still have to start off at midnight, after Dad has been at work; he comes home and has a nap and off we go, locking up and leaving Uncle John in charge of Nan's house. Susannah and I sit on each side of Nan in the back.

We have breakfast at a hamburger bar which we find incredibly glamorous, and after driving about a bit, Dad finds the bed and breakfast. As we sit outside, admiring the white gauze curtains, Dad comes out shaking his head.

"No good," he says to my mom. "They're charging much more than they said in the paper. We wouldn't have any money left at all, and we need lunch and dinner and petrol money even if we sit on the beach all day."

We can see that they are a bit worried and we fall really quiet. Dad has hardly slept at all and now he had to drive around finding somewhere we can afford. As it is Factory Fortnight most places are full. It is lunch time before we arrive at a place called Aveton Gifford and he asks an old man on the high street if the pub does bed and breakfast.

"Not the pub," says the old man who is about to change our lives, "but you could try the farm. She takes in paying guests sometimes." He gives my father some very complex instructions involving winding lanes, which confuses me even further, and in the early afternoon, we draw up in front of a rambling white building called Bigbury Court Farm.

Mrs Bricknell, the farmer's wife, a middle aged lady with horn rimmed glasses and set brown hair, isn't too keen; she has so much work to do anyway, but she seems to like something about my father.

"All right," she says. "I can do bed and breakfast and evening meal for the adults five shillings a night, and two and six each for the little girls."

And so in 1964 begin the most wonderful holidays I had ever known then or since.

Bigbury Court Farm is a working farm. It is a huge, white stone building with a thatched roof and a porch clustered with sweet smelling roses. A garden full of flowers surrounds the house, and stone walls mark where the fields begin. It is farmed by Mrs Bricknell's husband; they call him Tiny because he is so big. He is a genial man, with a ready smile and a soft Devon accent. Mrs Bricknell has brown hair and glasses; she always wears a flowered apron. They don't own the farm, she tells my mother, they farm it for a landlord and when they retire they will move into a bungalow in Totnes. The farm has masses of bedrooms; my sister and I share one, with huge beds made up with immaculate white linen and lavender smelling pillows and we have a bathroom of our very own with a bath set on claw legs. The running hot water is slow, says Mrs Bricknell apologetically, because it has to run uphill, but it is amazing to us because we don't have hot running water at home.

Breakfast and evening meals are served in the dining room, a huge sunny room downstairs opposite Mrs Bricknell's sitting room. She has a massive round dining table, set with shining stainless steel cutlery and folded linen napkins. There are two huge jugs on the table of orange and apple juice, and then she wheels in a trolley, covered in dishes with silver lids and sets the table with sausages, bacon, mushrooms, eggs and tomatoes, all steaming fresh from her kitchen range. It's such a treat for my mom and my nan not having to cook for two weeks. Evening meals are served in the same room; we have all the products of the farm, pork chops, lamb chops, sausages and veal, and on Sunday a huge round of roast beef with Yorkshire puddings, served with tureens of farm grown vegetables.

But what I really love is the vast array of puddings. We have one at home on Sunday but Mrs Bricknell serves one up every night, often with home-made clotted cream in a jug. My favourite is her lemon meringue, which I have never had, with its rich lemon interior and its topping of sugary white meringue.

Nan accompanies us every day, neat in her Lozells Rd tops and skirts. Some days we go down to the beach at Bigbury on Sea and sit there all day with our sandwich lunch. The beach is exciting because it faces an island, Burgh Island and the sea rushes in around the island, so we have to move quickly up the beach. Sometimes Dad takes us there at night because there is a pub, the Sailor's Arms, and an amusement arcade. One night, we travel over to the island in the sea tractor and sit outside the pub, The Pilchard, sipping scrumpy and lemonade, gazing at the imposing shape of the Art Deco hotel. Dad takes us for a walk around the island which is exciting, because it falls away steeply at the rear in a series of rocky cliffs.

Now that we have the car though, we can travel anywhere in Devon, making allowances for my travel sickness. We set off over the tidal road, which is exciting because if the tide isn't quite out Dad drives through the water, doing an emergency stop on the other side to test the brakes.

He takes us to Dartmoor, frightening us with the story of the Hairy Hands, to the point where I don't want to get out of the car, but I love Widecombe in the Moor, and we sing the ballad of Tom Pearce and Widecombe Fair in the car with great gusto.

We visit Plymouth and walk along the Hoe, and Dad tells us the story of Sir Francis Drake, finishing his game of bowls as the Armada heaves into view. We love this because Sir Francis Drake is on the telly and I have got a bit of a crush on him.

We visit Paignton for auld lang syne and Torquay with its waving palm trees, which my nan likes very much and Brixham, where Dad takes us out on a deep sea fishing trip. He doesn't catch any though, but we do see in the harbour, a basking shark hung up for all to see. I am frightened of it and hide my eyes.

Sometimes, friends of my parents accompany us on these holidays – the Atkins family, Frank and Elsie Collins with their daughters Marie and Vanessa, or the Nivens with their son Johnny who fancies my sister.

Devon is like another world. I have never seen anything like it; it seems right that it rhymes with Heaven. We seem to be in an enchanted world for two weeks every year where the sun is always out, and the sea is blue and sparkling and the countryside fresh and green and full of wildflowers. My sister and I, in our cotton sun frocks and shirts and shorts grow plump and brown, and my parents blossom, away from work for two weeks, relaxed, and full of good food and scrumpy. As for Nan, she has only ever been to Blackpool on a day trip and she is in Heaven.

"It's like another world," she says, shaking her head.

Birmingham seems smaller and grubbier when we get back late on the Saturday. But the rest of the holidays lie head for me and my sister; for Mom and Dad and Nan, it's back to work on the Monday.

16. Family Festivities

Things are beginning to change in the 1960s. The family has always lived in Aston, in council housing, even on the same street but now some of the younger members are beginning to buy houses and move out to really posh areas like Sutton Coldfield!

Weddings, christenings and funerals are the great family festivities. No-one in the family actually dies between 1953 and 1970, so that the era glows in my memory like amber without a fly trapped in it. No-one in the family even gets divorced. *Nobody* gets divorced.

Floss and Bert, my great aunt and uncle, still live next door to us with our cousins, David and Mark, but my Great Uncle Jack and Great Aunt Lil live over the law courts in a flat, because Uncle Jack is caretaker there. Nan takes us on a visit there and they have got a telephone in case Uncle Jack has to telephone the police. *Nobody* we know has a telephone. He gives us two old bakelite telephones to play with; they have little pull out drawers in the bottom to write telephone numbers on and we happily pretend to phone each other.

Nan also takes us on the bus to see her sister my Great Aunty Ada who lives in Erdington. She is a widow now, since 1947; her husband, our Great Uncle Joe, dropped dead after a very exciting football match between the Villa and the Spurs.

"The doctor warned him it was too much for his heart," she says, shaking her head and offering us some ice cold milk and custard tart with a crispy brown topping, or maybe a jam tart.

Aunty Eileen has been married for some years to Uncle Bernard. They have two children, my cousins Dean and Tracey and they live out in Solihull. When my mother takes us to see them, we have to get the bus into Birmingham and catch a train from the tiny Moor Street Station, which we love.

Uncle Charlie is married to Aunty Ann and they live out in Bearwood. I have a cousin Marie who has beautiful blonde hair always dressed in a bun on top of her head, which I, with my straight dark locks, really envy.

My dad doesn't really see many of his family, apart from his eldest brother, Uncle Albert. The family was fractured after the deaths of their parents and it has never really healed. My dad doesn't know any of his aunts and uncles or cousins. But Uncle Albert makes up for all that. He married a Black Country girl, my Aunty Mary, who is a tiny woman who laughs all the time, even though she is already in the grip of chronic arthritis. We have two cousins, Jim and Janet, and they live over in Wolverhampton. This is the dark side of the moon, but when my dad gets his car we can go over and see them. This requires organisation. My mum has to write to Aunty Mary and post it first class, asking her to phone the public call box at the end of our street at a certain time. Then my dad has to run down to the call box the day later, praying that no-one is using it, and wait for Uncle Albert to phone him, also from a public phone box.

Dad's eldest brother, Charlie, walks bent over double. He was injured in the war, whispers my mother. But Charlie is very jolly full of jokes and songs and Dad loves him. Charlie, who has no musical training, can play any piano. He marries a lovely widow called Lily and her daughters become our step cousins, Maureen and Eileen. Then at last he has his own little boy John, our cousin, with thick dark curls.

So the only members of the family left at home are Uncle Bill and Uncle John. Uncle John is only thirteen years older than me, and he works at the local bookie's. Uncle Bill is a lorry driver; he gets up at four o'clock every morning to drive long distances so he can get back early, have a nap, and go ballroom dancing in the evening. Uncle Bill adores his only nieces and he likes to sing snatches of song around the house: "Thank Heaven for little girls!"

My sister gets:

If you knew Susie, like I knew Susie, oh oh oh what a gal!

I get the very dreary *Amazing Grace*, but *Nothing could be finer than to be with Carolina in the morning!* is much jollier.

Anyway, Uncle Bill is getting married. His fiancée is a very beautiful blonde Irish girl called Margaret. She is part of a large Irish Brummie family brought up by their aunty because their parents died young. Like my Aunty Jean, she is a hairdresser, both of them started at the age of fourteen, sweeping up, washing hair, making tea, and then you go to college and take your City and Guilds. Now both of them have their own salons and they employ people.

Aunt Margaret and Uncle Bill have saved up £250 and they have put a deposit down on a house in Sutton Coldfield. We drive over to see it; it has three bedrooms, a kitchen and a lounge, but best of all it has a bathroom and inside toilet, running hot water and under floor central heating!

Uncle Bill also tells my parents that they have saved up enough money to go to Spain for a honeymoon. Nobody in the family has ever been abroad, except on National Service and they are having something called a package holiday.

The only fly in this ointment is that Aunty Margaret is a Catholic and they are getting married in the Catholic Church. Because everyone loves Aunty Margaret, my nan has put aside her suspicions about the Catholic Church, but what is really sad is that my sister and I can't be bridesmaids. We are Church of England, and the Catholic Church won't allow it.

"I'll make sure that they look as pretty as bridesmaids," says my mother.

On the great day, my mother and my nan go up to Marjorie's to have their hair specially set. My mother's beehive is the most sophisticated she has yet had, but my nan just has a blue rinse because she is going grey. Even better than that, we have our hair done too! We have it shampooed and then Marjorie puts rollers in (which we don't like, they stick into our heads and are fastened with huge grips) and then we sit under the massive hairdryers. Even with all this effort, all she can do is give me a slight curl under, like a page boy, but my sister's curls are dressed atop her head, and Marjorie carefully fits hairbands made out of white silk roses on each of us.

"Just like a bridesmaid," says Nan consolingly.

We went to the washing baths on Friday night so we are all beautifully clean. My sister and I have matching orange skirts and jackets, with a white blouse underneath, and we have white socks with lace edging and white silken slippers. My mother is resplendent in peach lace and my grandmother in a matching powder blue hat and coat. And so we all beam out from the wedding photograph, led by the family matriarch, my grandmother, a working class Aston family, dressed to the nines, a fly preserved in the amber nugget of time.

My sister and I are somewhat consoled by the presents Uncle Bill brings back from Spain; castanets, fans, lacy shawls and pretty Spanish dolls, and for a long time Spanish Lady is our favourite game.

In the autumn of 1964, Uncle John gets engaged to be married. He likes to go up to the nightclubs in Birmingham and he brings all his pretty girlfriends home for my nan to approve. They always have blonde hair and wear beautiful clothes. Then he gets engaged to the prettiest of all, our aunt to be, June. Very beautiful she is, *"like* Dusty Springfield," says my dad admiringly, with her lacquered blonde bob, her eye make up, her fashionable clothes and her high heeled shoes; she is a very efficient supervisor at Pertemps staff agency in the Rotunda and sometimes she takes me and my sister there for a treat.

Anyway, the best bit about all this is that we are going to be bridesmaids! At last! My mother takes us on the bus to the dressmaker, all the way over in Castle Vale where June lives. But she doesn't like the dresses at all.

"They're *white,*" she complains to my grandmother, "and so plain as well!"

She likes our turquoise sashes better, and the wreaths of white flowers stitched onto turquoise bands in our hair, which is to be dressed by Marjorie just as it was for Uncle Bill's wedding. We have little posies of silk flowers too. A great white limousine arrives to take us to the church; it is early spring, but it is snowing and at the last minute the dressmaker has provided us with little fur jackets and muffs to wear, but we are so worried about carrying the train right that we don't notice the cold.

The reception is at the Co-op, as nearly everyone has it there; big tables set out with an array of food, but it's a cold buffet this time where Uncle Bill had a hot meal. My sister and I especially enjoy the sausage rolls, the jelly and the trifle; it's just boring that my mother says we must eat our sandwiches first. But we all get a big slice of iced wedding cake, wrapped up in a silver edged napkin to take home.

17. Sound and Vision

My parents have a small twelve inch screen black and white TV, they have a radio and they have a record player. The record player stands on four legs; it takes six singles or one LP at a time, but always more than one disc drops down when you set the playtime at 33 or 78. Many of their records are labelled His Master's Voice; the picture of the dog gazing at the gramophone makes me cry, because my dad tells us he is listening to his dead master's voice.

My nan has been listening to the radio since the nineteen twenties, and because of that she sounds just like a BBC announcer, *"This ees the Bee Bee Cee."*

My parents also have a small silver radio with a tuning dial and a push up aerial. It is permanently tuned to the Light Programme. My parents think that the Third Programme and the Home Service are 'la di da'. My mother listens every day to the exciting saga of *Mrs Dale's Diary*, although my nan prefers *The Archers*; she has never got over the unfortunate death of Grace Archer.

"It was like losing a member of the family," she sighs.

For my sister and I, the radio means *Listen with Mother*, although there are some songs we like to hear, like Danny Kaye singing the *Ugly Duckling*. We don't like *Hang Down Your Head, Tom Dooley* because it is so sad, and the *Laughing Policeman* makes me cry, it is so frightening! *Big Bad John* makes us think of Uncle John, who is over six foot. But we do love the adventures of *The Clitheroe Kid* and his slightly dim friend, Alfie.

My mother still laments the demise of *Dick Barton – Special Agent*. "I used to run home every day after work to listen to it!"

Friday night is always *Music Night*, and Sunday afternoon means *World Wide Family Favourites*, flowed by the Shipping News. One marks the beginning of the weekend, and the other the end.

In 1960 my parents decide to buy a television, which means that they draw their savings out of the Post Office and buy a TV from Rumbelow's on the

New Town Row, but they do use the Never Never to buy one for my nan; she has to take her book and her payment into Rumbelow's every week and get it stamped. The TV is black and white with a twelve inch screen and it sits in an alcove next to the fire which was once the space for the oven before the cellar door became the kitchen area.

The flickering black and white images are the earliest TV my sister and I remember. We love the opening flower at the beginning of *Watch with Mother*, which we now only see in the holidays, and my mother likes the programme that follows it, *Lunchbox* with Noelle Gordon. We also love Tingha and Tucka, the two little koala bears with auntie Jean Morton, Pinky and Perky the pigs, and above all Sooty and Sweep with Uncle Harry Corbett.

But now that my sister and I are at school, we love the early evening programmes, which all seem to be about noble heroes saving us from dastardly foreigners. Roger Moore as *Ivanhoe*! Conrad Phillips as *William Tell*! *The Adventures of Sir Francis Drake*, week after week battling the machinations of the Spanish Ambassador and Philip of Spain! Richard Greene as Robin Hood, battling Prince John and the Sheriff of Nottingham!

My dad rather fancies Maid Marian and Mrs Tell so he watches them with us.

Even better than these noble heroes, we enjoy anything that is animated. The first puppet show we can remember is *Torchy the Battery Boy*, but this is soon replaced in our affections by the exciting adventures of Mike Mercury in *Supercar*, and then by *Fireball XL5* with Steve Zodiac, and we want to be Venus, his glamorous blonde sidekick.

Our favourite is the last (at least for us) in this sequence, *Thunderbirds*. I am in love with Scott Tracy (pilot of Thunderbird 1) and my sister is in love with Virgil (pilot of No 2) because he is a bit artistic in his smock and beret as he occasionally daubs away at a painting. We want to *marry* them when we grow up, we tell our father, who has a fit laughing.

"If you do," he wheezes between guffaws, "your children will be logs!"

We have a new heroine now: Lady Penelope with her blonde bob (she looks like Aunty June), her beautiful clothes, her cut glass accent, her independence, and best of all her pink Rolls Royce, driven by Parker, her devoted chauffeur who can do *anything*, and spends much of the programme obediently saying "Yus, m' lady".

For a short time, I have an extra comic called *Lady Penelope*.

"Parker is an *ideal* man," reflects my mother. "He can do anything and he's obedient!"

Conscientiously, she tries to get us interested in *Blue Peter*, but we think it dull and don't want to make things out of sticky back plastic or cornflakes packets, although we do like Petra the dog. But Johnny Morris in *Animal Magic* is a much better animal programme.

Friday of course means that it is five o'clock and it is *Crackerjack!* My sister and I have hysterics at the antics of Leslie Crowther and Peter Glaze.

My parents like cop shows and legal drama, like *Gideon's Way*, *No Hiding Place*, *Z Cars* and *Perry Mason*. They scorn soap operas because my father says they are "opiate for the masses," spouting from his Trades Union classes, and my mother says they show people who aren't trying to better themselves in any way.

They also enjoy dramas, like *Play for Today*, *Armchair Theatre* and *The Wednesday Play*, which on the whole we don't watch, because they are on when we are in bed.

One Wednesday evening in November 1966, we hear them coming up to bed after *The Wednesday Play*. We can hear them talking in whispers on the stairs.

"Shocking ..."

"It was just like us .... It could happen to anyone ..."

"Someone ought to help ... to do something ..."

"Dad, what were you talking about in the night?" I ask in the morning.

He gives me a sideways glance and says shortly:

"A play called *Cathy Come Home*."

On a lighter note, my parents love comedy, especially Morecambe and Wise, and my father is reduced to tears by the antics of Phil Silvers as Sergeant Bilko. The jokes are so fast on this, that we don't quite get them, like our favourite American cartoon, *Top Cat*. My father says this is called wisecracking and is American.

We love watching comedies together with them, programmes that we can all watch such as *Steptoe and Son*, *The Army Game* and *Bootsie and Snudge*. We enjoy quiz programmes as well; Michael Miles in *Double Your Money* and Hughie Green in *Take your Pick*. "Take the money! Open the box!" we yell at the screen, as though they can *hear* us.

Neither my mother nor my grandmother like costume dramas, although they are pinned to the sofa by a Sunday night drama called *The Forsyte Saga*. They have to wait till it is on BBC One as we don't have BBC Two.

"That nasty Irene," says my nan.

"No woman deserves that, though," says my mother, discreetly edging us out of the room as Soames rips off Irene's bodice.

As my sister and I spend most of our evenings and Saturday with Dad, while Mom is working or shopping, our viewing tastes are determined by his. Of course, we get to see *Grandstand* and *Match of the Day* – the football results as announced on the tickertape are thrilling – but we also watch every Western on TV because that's what he likes: *Bonanza*, *Rawhide*, *Maverick*, *Sugarfoot*, and *Champion the Wonder Horse*, galloping across the plain.

There are a few series on television which are foreign, though we don't know it. We love *Robinson Crusoe*, which is French with its strange, sad music, and *White Horses*, which is German; we try to sing along with the theme music but we can never quite catch all the words. It takes us years to realise why the characters' mouths don't synchronise with what they are actually saying.

My sister and I hate the news. It is boring and sad. But my parents love it. They listen, shocked, as Sir Winston Churchill's death is announced and they follow the grainy black and white footage of the funeral on a dark day in January 1965. My mother points out to me the great cranes dipping in salute as the coffin makes its way along the Thames.

My sister and I are more upset by the death of Walt Disney in 1966, as we think there won't be any more Disney films, but my mother says consolingly that Walt has a brother Roy who looks *just* like him and he will carry on the studio.

In November 1963, my mother buys the TV Times as usual, and tell us that there is a going to be an exciting new serial for children, called *Dr Who*, starting on the Saturday. My sister and I look at the photos of the doctor, who looks a bit frightening, but agree it might be worth giving a whirl.

On the Friday afternoon, when my mother picks us up from school, we are startled to see that her eyes are red with weeping.

"They shot President Kennedy!"

When my father gets home, he immediately puts on the TV and they are glued to it all night. They *loved* President Kennedy. We don't see *Dr Who* on Saturday – my parents think it is inappropriate, and in fact we never really take to it as the Daleks are so frightening and they might land on Earth and take us over.

"Don't worry," says my father consolingly when I confide this. "It rains so much in England that the Daleks would just rust up, and anyway we can just go upstairs and they can't get us there."

My grandmother also loves her little black and white TV, and with her, we watch programmes starring her favourite actors, such as *Danger Man*, *The Avengers*, and *The Saint*.

"I have four favourites," she says dreamily. "An Englishman, a Scotchman, an Irishman and a Welshman." She means Roger Moore, Sean Connery, Patrick MacGoohan and Richard Burton.

My father has other favourites apart from Maid Marian and Mrs Tell: Adrienne Corri, Barbara Murray in *The Power Game*, to which my parents are addicted, and Nyree Dawn Porter as Irene. Their every appearance on the screen is punctuated by the same comment:

"Isn't she beautiful?"

On Saturday nights, we all cuddle up on the green sofa, watching the (politically incorrect) *Black and White Minstrels* together. My sister and I are a bit bored by it as it is all singing, but my parents love the songs. They are inspired enough to go all the way to the Birmingham Hippodrome to buy tickets for the Minstrels' stage show for us. It is our very first ever visit to the theatre (my parents haven't been here since they saw *Kismet* way back in the fifties with the youth club), and we are dressed in our best party frocks and shoes. We love the gleaming chandeliers, the gilt seats and the velvet curtain, and the little tub of vanilla ice cream with a spoon which my father treats us all to in the interval, and the show isn't as boring as we feared because there is also a magician and a man with a troupe of performing poodles!

One summer day in 1966, my father moves the sofa round so it faces the television, and stations himself in front of it at one o'clock with a crate of Davenport's. He announces that this is the most important day in English football; the 1966 World Cup Final between England and West Germany, and we are *all* going to watch it; this is history!

I can just about remember 1962; 1966 is in England and my father has been glued to every match, marvelling at the talents of Eusebio and Pele. Like every other English person, he has taken to his heart plucky little underdogs North Korea, in their match against the mighty Portugal.

But now it is the final and it is us. My mother makes us sausage sandwiches to eat while watching it and puts Golden Wonder into a big bowl. I peer out of the door into the street; nobody about at all, and the sound of televisions and radios coming from every house.

The grainy pictures on our black and white telly don't stop us from thrilling to the match, watched on the Beeb as my dad thinks their sports coverage is better. Of course, we don't know that England are in red, and my mother is cross: "They should be in white!"

My sister and I are heartbroken when West Germany pull back to 2 – 2 but my dad says simply:

"In Sir Alf we trust." Not to mention Bobby Moore *et al.*

The room explodes when Geoff Hurst hits his third and fourth ... "Some people are on the pitch ... they think it's all over ... it is now!"

My mother sighs over the Queen, such a lady in her white gloves, as she hands Bobby Moore the trophy. My sister and I love the toothless Nobby Stiles, dancing all over the turf with the cup.

"Never mind," says my dad consolingly. "We'll win it again in 1970. This is the start of a great era in English football!"

One bright autumn Saturday morning in 1962, my mother is walking up the Lozells Rd, swinging her shopping bag, when she stops to look in the window of the record shop. They have just bought from Rumbelow's on the Newtown Rd a small record player, which can take six singles at a time (although several often drop down together), and they are thinking of starting a record collection.

In the centre of the window is the sleeve of a new single: *Love Me Do*, with a painting of four young men in smart grey suits, but this is surrounded by photographs of these same young men, with glossy hair and wide smiles.

My mother stares. She looks again. One face in particular catches her attention: the face of the one called John Lennon. She cannot stop looking at him as he gazes out cheekily at her.

She walks straight in and buys the single without even hearing it on the radio first. Later that day, as my father carefully positions it on the turntable and drops the needles, we hear for the very first time the sound of The Beatles.

My mother buys every Beatles single as it comes out.

"They'll be worth a mint one day!" she says.

She scans the *Daily Mirror* every day, looking for photographs of them, and she sends off to the Beatles official fan club for (black and white) photographs for us to paste into our autograph albums. And then sometimes they are on the telly, mainly news film of them arriving or departing concerts, with the police pushing back thousands of screaming and hysterical fans. My mother takes us to see *A Hard Day's Night* (also in black and white) at the Orient Cinema, where we see our heroes larger than life on the screen. Ah, but they are beautiful, with their glossy hair – the moptops – their long-lashed eyes, their smart suits, their fashionable high heeled boots – Chelsea boots – and their wit and understanding.

Of course, we all have favourites; John for my mother, who never quite gets over that first moment of seeing his photograph, the boyish Paul for my sister, and George for me, because he seems moody and mysterious. My father says with a laugh that means he will have to like Ringo best, but in fact he does think that Ringo is the best actor and has the wittiest way with a line.

"How can such young men know such things," says my father, shaking his head as he listens to *Eleanor Rigby* on the radio.

"The Beatles *are* the Sixties," he adds. "It's something we gave to the world that was good and that everybody loved and it made them all happy."

He says to my mother:

"Once Harold Wilson and The Beatles are gone, the Sixties are over."

Of course, now that they have a record player, The Beatles are not the only singles that they buy. They love Helen Shapiro and Dusty Springfield, the epitome of Sixties beauty with their lacquered bobs and beehives, their pretty frocks and their heavy eye make up (but they don't like Cilla Black, Petula Clark or Lulu). We have singles by Gerry and the Pacemakers, the Swinging Blue Jeans, the Animals, The Trogs, the Kinks, and Freddie and the Dreamers (but not The Rolling Stones; my mother doesn't like them, they are the bad boys to The Beatles' cleancut reputation).

My father loves Shirley Bassey, and my mother and nan, Tom Jones.

"The Welsh can certainly sing!" says my mother, carefully extracting *It's Not Unusual* from its wrapper.

On Saturday morning, our house echoes to the Sounds of the Sixties, as my sister and I dance The Twist, to the music coming from our parents' record player, short skirts swinging, and it seems, if you go outside, that the same music seems to echo from every house.

"There'll never be anything ever like it in the world again," says my father. "The one era when everyone in the world listened to our music and it made them feel happy."

18. The Silver Screen

The family have been going to "the pictures" since the cinemas have been built. The cinemas of Birmingham are picture palaces, just as the pubs, like the Barton's Arms, are gin palaces and the state schools are cathedrals of learning, and the washing baths are temples of cleanliness and our parks, with their football pitches, their cricket pavilions and their brass band stands, are places of wonder. The state gave them to the working classes, and the state will take them away.

By the Sixties, some of the local cinemas have already closed: the Globe, the Aston Hippodrome (where Laurel and Hardy used to play, staying at the Barton's Arms), the Newtown Palace and The Lozells Picture House.

My nan used to go to The Globe to see Rudolf Valentino.

"Not just The Globe," she says. "I would get the *Evening Mail* on Friday and look at the cinema listings, and wherever there was a Valentino film playing, I would get the bus there to see it."

I think my grandmother has a taste for foreign glamour. After the death of Valentino, she is captivated by the twinkly Gallic charm of Maurice Chevalier, starring in early musicals with Jeanette Macdonald. He disappears off the screen in the mid nineteen thirties, but she is thrilled when twenty years later, he reappears in *Gigi*, charm undimmed.

When Maurice Chevalier disappears off the screen, she develops a passion for the French actor Charles Boyer. One afternoon, we find her glued to the TV screen, watching him die beautifully in his white ruffled shirt against a stack of pillows as Bette Davis weeps over him in *All This and Heaven Too*.

After Charles Boyer, she develops a liking for Herbert Lom, now mainly to be seen in the *Pink Panther* films, which is something we can all go and see together, like James Bond, at the Odeon Birmingham. This is the very first cinema my sister and I ever go to, to see our first film, *Snow White and the Seven Dwarfs*, at Christmas 1962. We are terrified by the witch, but we love the sparkling jewel mine, just as the Christmas lights of Birmingham are sparkling the whole length of New Street, up the huge Christmas tree in Victoria Square, a gift from the people of Norway.

We always go to the Odeon to see a Disney film, so here we see *Bambi, Cinderella, Sleeping Beauty,* and *The Lady and the Tramp*, which my parents love because of the voice of Peggy Lee. My sister disgraces herself by bursting into tears at the death of Bambi's mother, and my embarrassed father has to carry her out. But when we go to see *Born Free*, with Elsa the lioness, he is the one who is sobbing.

"It was the music," he says apologetically.

We love *Mary Poppins*, and for months afterwards it is our favourite game; I am Mary, Cherie next door is Bert, and my sister is Jane and Michael. We raid our dressing up box of my mother's old clothes for costume, and pirouette across the yard singing *Chim Chim Cheree* while my father looks on and laughs.

My parents' great cinema going days were the fifties, when they went to see every musical they could. The Villa Cross on the Lozells Rd shows old musicals every Saturday and Sunday afternoon, and they take us up there. It is a beautiful building with a rose window like you see in a church, and here we enjoy *Seven Brides for Seven Brothers, Kiss Me Kate,* and *Singin' in the Rain*, and in full colour too!

For several weeks in a row they show musicals associated with fairy tales, and so we enjoy *Tom Thumb, The Wonderful World of the Brothers Grimm,* which has some quite frightening fantasy sequences which make us hide our eyes, and *Hans Christian Andersen*, with Danny Kaye, so at last we see the man who sings all the songs we love to hear on the radio. Best if all is *The Wizard of Oz* with Judy Garland, my mother's favourite film star, and it starts off in black and white just like our telly and then bursts into glorious colour!

Even closer to us is the Orient Cinema, halfway up the hill to Six Ways, and so called because it has fanciful Eastern décor. Sometimes we go to the Saturday Morning Kids' club with David and Mark, where they try to sell us members' badges, but we don't want them as they cost sixpence. But they only ever show the same film over and over, a black and white version of *Five on a Treasure Island*, and it breaks every week at the same point so we never see the end, and all the kids boo and stamp their feet. When this happens, the manager hurriedly sends out an entertainer, like a magician, which is much better.

We also boo the short educational films they show which you get before the main film – things about the post office or British Rail which are really boring.

My mother takes us to see anything she wants to see which usually has an A certificate. In this way we see *Cleopatra*, because my mother adores Elizabeth Taylor and my mum and my nan adore Richard Burton.

"Such a wonderful voice, as though he were speaking through something," sighs my mum.

The biggest and grandest cinema in Birmingham is the Gaumont, where we never go, because it is so expensive. However, in 1965, a musical called *The Sound of Music* is released, and my parents think wistfully that they would like to see it at the Gaumont as the screen is so big. My father doesn't do the pools, but he does do *Spot the Ball* in the *Birmingham Evening Mail* every week. It is a blurry, grainy picture of a football match with the ball removed and you have to put crosses where you think the ball might be.

One Saturday night he picks up his *Mail* from Cooper's and comes up the entry to my nan's where we are all sitting with her watching the football results on *Grandstand*, hoping that the Villa have won. Dad sits at the table, perusing the results of last week's *Spot the Ball*, published in the paper every Saturday night.

Suddenly, he looks up, his face ruddier than ever.

"I've won!" he says beaming.

There it is, his name in print. Mr W A Holte, *fifty pounds!!!*

This is unbelievable; the family has never known anything like this! My nan puts on the kettle and passes round Peter Stuyvesants while my dad plans aloud what he is going to do with this windfall.

Chocolates for all the women in the family, a new pair of glasses for my nan so she doesn't have to have NHS frames, and best of all, he is going to take us to see *The Sound of Music* at the Gaumont!

Dad has to go up the *Mail* offices to collect his winnings, and he goes straight over to the Gaumont and buys three five shilling and two two and sixpenny tickets – the very best in the house!

On the appointed night, we can skip the queue because we have got tickets, and even better, Dad splashes out on a five shillings programme with pictures of Julie Andrews, Christopher Plummer and the seven von Trapp children. The film, which we love, is so long that there is an interval, and we all get a choc ice to eat from the lady who walks around with a little lit up tray, and my sister and I get a refreshing Kia Ora.

The Sound of Music runs in Birmingham for years, and we do go and see it again, but nothing ever captures the magic of that first time.

I decide I want to be an usherette in a cinema; you get to wear a smart uniform with a hat and see all the films free of charge.

19. In Sickness and in Health

Thank Heavens for the NHS say my parents and my nan, remembering with a shudder the bad old days before it, when women on the street died in childbirth, and my father's mother died screaming in pain from stomach cancer, because the family couldn't afford a doctor.

The NHS is Dr Carolan, in his small surgery in a terraced house, coughing as he puffs on his cigarette and writes you a prescription. As nobody has a phone, you can't call him to make an appointment; you simply turn up in the morning or the evening and sit in the overcrowded waiting room where everybody is smoking.

The NHS is now God; it promises immortality just as the Church used to.

My parents are splendidly healthy, but my nan is fragile; she has had a heart operation. All the same, all three think that the NHS is really only there to be bothered if you are really ill, and they have a whole range of home grown remedies dating from before the war.

My mother regards it as a personal insult that my sister suffers from bronchitis and I suffer from catarrh and she doesn't connect it with the dampness of the house, the prevalence of smoking, or the thick Birmingham smog. We have three square meals a day and plenty of fresh air and exercise; what more can we want?

She is extremely cross when the school nurse sends home a letter saying we are too small, too thin and cough too much. She goes into battle; we are given a spoon of cod liver oil (which we hate) and a spoon of Delrosa (which we love, it's so sweet) every morning. My sister, in addition, is made to drink a pint of pasteurised milk every day.

A lady from the council comes round to see my mother to discuss whether my sister should be sent to one of Birmingham's open air schools.

"Well, I'd rather she died at home than lived in one of those," says my mother gloomily, rather as my nan once refused to have her children evacuated, saying it was better for them to die together as a family than live separated in the country. The working classes have little choice, and the choices they do have are often terrible.

All the same, our cousin Mark is sent off for a month to an open air school in Herefordshire. Floss and Bert try and visit him one Saturday; they get the train to Hereford, then a bus and a long walk down a country lane, but when they get there, he is asleep and the staff won't let them see him.

When we cough, my mother spoons Gee's Linctus, which we rather like, into us. When I have pleurisy, my nan puts a bag of hot sand onto my back. Colds, stomach aches and headaches are treated with a dose of Junior Aspro. Whooping cough, influenza and pneumonia might mean a home visit from the doctor as we lie stretched out on the sofa in the living room, covered with a blanket – the bedroom is too cold. Apart from being ill we like this, because my mother has the radio on and I can read my books all day. One Christmas, my cold turns into the flu which my mother seems to regard as another personal insult, but Dr Carolan says I must stay at home till after Christmas. My mother puts the Christmas tree up early to amuse me and I lie there making up stories about the angels and snowmen and elves which make up the decorations. But my parents have never missed a day off work through illness, and they don't really think we should miss days off school. So on the whole my sister and I prefer not to be off, as their displeasure is apparent. There are kids who are off at school and the Truant Officer is sent out for them, but if we are off, my mother either walks up to tell Mrs Wardell, or posts a note which they will get by lunchtime.

My mother is a stickler for taking us for our inoculations – she remembers the bad old days when people died of cholera, diphtheria and tetanus, indeed anything – but many of these take place at school. We all queue up for the polio jab, which is much nastier than the previous inoculations, a spoonful of orange juice and a lump of sugar, and most of the kids are screaming.

My mother wishes there was an inoculation for tuberculosis and German measles. She can remember people dying of TB in the 1930s – there was no cure and the working classes were not sent off to the fresh air hospitals in the countryside. But she worries even more about the German measles, because there is a poor old deformed man on the street whose mother caught German measles while she was pregnant.

"They must be immune to it," says my mother indignantly after she exposes us to everyone she knows who gets German measles, even David and Mark on their sickbeds, and we remain German measles free. To her annoyance, we do get measles and chickenpox, and despite her best efforts in swabbing us with calomel, I scratch my spots which turn septic.

"They have to come off," says Dr Carolan and he comes round to the house to cut them off with a small knife while my mother and nan hold me down, leaving scars I bear to this day.

Germolene comes out for any cuts or bruises, and for my rather spectacular boils, my mother applies an evil smelling ointment called Black Jack. My mouth ulcers are treated with honey; "Don't lick it off!"

Although the family on the whole tries to avoid using the doctor's, they are very glad of the services of the dentist, Mr Moon, who operates from a little terraced house on the corner in Witton. The state of the working classes' teeth is notorious and there are older people on our street who have no teeth at all. When their teeth became painful and rotten, they tied a string to it, knotted the other end to the door, and got someone to slam it.

My grandmother has terrible teeth – long and yellow and rotting. My parents' teeth are yellowing and crossed, and when they become painful they troop off to Mr Moon's.

"They all have to come out – too far gone," he says to my grandmother. He puts her out using the gas, and fits her with brand new dentures, top and bottom, which she takes out every night and soaks in pink Steradent.

My parent's teeth aren't so far gone. Mr Moon can't do anything about them having inherited yellowing teeth apart from telling them to brush with Colgate, but he does remove some excess back teeth from their overcrowded mouths, and replace their crossed front teeth with crowns, which are curiously whiter than the rest of their teeth.

My sister and have lovely pearly baby teeth, so my mother is furious when these fall out and are replaced with the family teeth – excess, yellowing, crossed, elongated. She takes me straight off to see Mr Moon, who says gravely that he must remove the excess teeth and I must wear a brace to straighten the rest. He will put me on the waiting list for the Birmingham Dental Hospital, which is two years so it is going to be when I am at secondary school, but he will remove the excess teeth himself.

On the appointed day, as neither my mother or my grandmother can bear to see my suffering, my father takes me down to Mr Moon as soon as he gets in from work.

"Be brave," he admonishes me as we drive up to Six Ways, because I am pale and sick with horror.

Mr Moon also tells me to be brave as he fits the gas mask over my face, but I can't stand it – it causes me to panic, to kick and wave my arms, even as I lose consciousness and fall into a dystopian nightmare of a curiously evil and grinning Mr Moon chasing after me. When I wake up, I am screaming and my mouth is covered with blood and then I burst into tears, which disconcerts my dad, because on the whole I don't cry. Embarrassed, he escorts me, a sobbing husk, out into the cold night air and now my gums are so sore that I can't eat or drink a thing.

In all the years that I have been at school, I have tried to sit closer and closer every year to the blackboard, because it's a bit of a blur if I sit further back.

It is Mrs Burton who notices that I am squinting. She marches me off to the school nurse, who calls in on a weekly basis. Usually, she is dealing with the nit epidemic which periodically sweeps the school; my mother deals with this by washing our hair in kerosene and combing it with a fine toothed plastic comb, which makes us wince.

The school nurse sends a note home to my parents; I need to see an optician. My parents are appalled. They have twenty/twenty vision.

"Although Mom has glasses now and David Burke has them for reading," reflects my mother, and indeed my cousin David sports little NHS blue frames.

"You remember that time we were in the country, and I said, 'Look at that pig in that field!' and she said '*What* field?' I think we should have noticed *then*," rejoins my dad.

My father takes me up on Saturday morning to Cox's Opticians, which is set in a terraced house off Six Ways. I sit in the tiny waiting room, warmed with a popping gas fire, while my father fills in numerous NHS forms.

Mr Cox is small and cheerful; he has curly hair and wears a tweed jacket, cord trousers and thick frames. He positions me on a high chair in front of a big chart fixed to the wall and asks me to read off it; I do about three lines and stop. Then he puts the light out and puts some very heavy and uncomfortable frames onto my nose, into which he slips little lenses. I have to look at the chart which is now illuminated and read off it, and compare the brightness of various green and red lights. I rather enjoy doing this, but afterwards Mr Cox gravely explains to my father that I am very short sighted and require glasses, so I have failed the test.

"Lenses are free and you can have NHS frames which are free also," he explains.

Up till now, I have been quite pleased at being short sighted; I am *different*. But as Mr Cox lifts up the small round pink NHS frames, I am in shock. The kids at school will know! I lift my agonised eyes up to my dad and he, maybe remembering his experiences at school with his *Daily Mail* boots, rises magnificently to the occasion.

"We'll go private," he says loftily.

Mr Cox takes us into a small room full of trays and trays of empty frames. I pick a strawberry coloured pair costing 12/6d, and Mr Cox says they will be ready in a week. When we pick them up, in a flowery plastic case, I take them proudly into school to show Mrs Burton.

"It's all that reading, affecting her sight," sniffs my mother.

20. Playtime

My mother thinks that all well brought up children should have plenty of fresh air and exercise and be out of the house at least two hours a day. However, when it is raining or foggy, even she acknowledges that we can't go out.

The house is small and our bedroom has no fire and is cold so this means playing in the living room. Of course I have my books and my sister has her jigsaw puzzles, which she has been doing ever since I went to school. We have a wide range of colouring books, Caran d'Ache pencils, and lovely smelling wax crayons which my mother has bought us from The House That Jack Built, but she gets cross when we suck them.

We have little painting boxes with brushes; my mother gives us a jam jar of water and ties little aprons onto us as I try to paint the ballet dancers in my library book.

We have dolls to play with too. I am senior sister, so I have the senior doll, Christina Ann, who has brown hair and blue eyes. My only other doll has platinum hair and is a gift from my parents.

"Call her Snow White!" says my mother.

"Call her Snow Drop!" says my father.

I have this odd idea that if I pick one name I will hurt the other, so I call the poor doll Snow White Snow Drop.

My sister's first doll was Bessy, a plastic baby doll that was her first Christmas present in 1958 when she was only three months old. She has a golden haired doll called Goldilocks and a real beauty called Lisa, which I envy because Lisa has long hair and my sister can brush it with a special soft brush with a daisy on it.

We dress the dolls in little dresses bought by my mother, and cardigans knitted by Floss which are a work of art in themselves and we take them for walks in the dolls' prams which my parents saved up a whole year for, and which are kept in one of the collection of ramshackle sheds in the yard. We dress up to do this and my mother gives us some of her old high heeled shoes to clack around in so we look really grown up.

The dolls all sit on a pouffe in our bedroom, gazing over us. Then one day my mother, noticing that my sister has been absent from the living room for some time, puffs all the way upstairs.

She finds my sister tearful and defiant, with my father's penknife in her hand, and surrounded by a collection of bits of blue glass. *She has gouged out the eyes of all the dolls.*

"I woke up in the night and they were staring at me!" she wails.

More to our taste are our selection of teddy bears and soft toys, bought mainly at jumble sales, although I do have a beautiful giraffe, called Gerry, made out of sponge and bought for me by Uncle Bill. But sadly he is crumbling away slowly.

We have a squeaky pig called Porky, a genial stuffed dog called Rex, a poodle with the original name of Poody, two teddy bears called Janet and Susan, dressed in frocks knitted by Floss, and I have Sweety, a tiny knitted teddy purchased for threepence by my mother at the school jumble sale. We sing to our teddies at night, as they lie ranged in the bed next to us (we always have them in bed or their feelings might be hurt) and we make up all sorts of wonderful adventures for them.

But best of all we like to play outside and the back yard, indeed the street, is our playground, as hardly any cars pass down the street and the boys play football in it.

"Look after the bab," says my mother to me.

"Look after the little girls," says Floss to David and Mark, words all of us remember fifty years later when they are all gone.

My sister and I have roller skates, with rubber wheels and laces which tie up over our toes. We soon wear the wheels out as we zoom over the bricked over part of the yard. We have scooters which we pedal along the street, and we have the bikes which our parents bought from the Burlington catalogue one Christmas. We love to take them up to the top of the street where it meets the Lozells Rd and launch ourselves down the hill, screaming with delight.

We have a pogo stick which I never really master; I take a couple of bounces and I fall off.

With a stick of chalk, we make a grid for hopscotch with Cherie next door; we compete with our skipping ropes, seeing who can skip the longest. My father brings us plastic hula hoops and we spin them around us, seeing who can hula the longest. He rigs up an impromptu tennis net with a rope, and we play tennis for hours with the rackets and balls I got at the Lucas's Christmas party.

But these are our girlish pursuits. What we really like is to run about with David and Mark and their Gang; David is Leader of the Gang, Mark is vice captain and we, presumably, are the gang molls.

Much to the annoyance of my mother, grandmother and Floss, the Gang nearly always assembles in our yard, but this is maybe due to the influence of Uncle John, not much older than a schoolboy himself. He plays cricket for Warwickshire Schoolboys, and my nan and my mom have some ado boiling his whites every Monday to get out the grass stains and dirt, but it is worth it as they swoon with admiration as he goes off in his dazzling whites, with his bat tucked under his arm and his ball in his pocket.

He rigs up some stumps in the yard, made out of an old broomstick, and teaches the Gang how to play, but we nearly always end up as fielders as Uncle John does not think girls can bat or bowl. When he divides the Gang up into two teams for football, with a plastic ball and four heaps of coats for goals, we have to be the referees. We find this very unfair. But we are allowed to play rounders, as the Gang think this is more suitable for girls. Many a ball disappears into the large, empty window of the factory, there to stay till it is demolished.

The Gang plays hide and seek in the yard. One of the Gang hides his eyes and counts to ten and we rush off to hide; when he is ready to come and find us, he yells, "Coming!" you can win the game by getting back to base before him and yelling "Acky acky acky!"

One time, my sister is seeker and I rush down to the house and up the stairs and hide under my parents' bed where there is a space next to the wall. I lie with my eyes closed, listening out; I hear the door open and footsteps cross the room. How could she be so quick? I roll into a ball and keep still.

Nothing happens. I wait a few minutes and then pop my head up, ready to make a run. *Nobody is in the room* and I jump up and run as fast as I can down to the living room.

"Dad," I sob, "I heard a ghost!"

He hears me out, and says consolingly:

"You know, the walls of these houses are very thin. You just heard Floss next door."

But to my mother he says privately:

"You know the old lady who used to live here .... That was her bedroom."

Sometimes we cross the road to play on the old bomb peck as we call it, where half the street was destroyed during the war. They did not rebuild the houses because they are planning to demolish the street and build a new council estate. Huge piles of dirt make hills and mountains on which we can play Explorers, and a big pile of abandoned planks becomes a pirate ship, or maybe a Treasure Island, and David and Mark make us bows and arrows out of twigs and string.

One day we find an old tin bath dumped on top of the planks, and we have a wonderful day sliding down them in it, pretending that we are sledging. The drop is almost vertical, but luckily the grown ups can't see.

Another time, we are not so lucky.

One day Floss brings an old pram up the yard, to the space for the pile of rubbish between the sheds.

"Can we have that?" asks David.

Floss is suspicious. "What for?"

"To make a go kart," says David, which seems fine, so she nods and the Gang go off and fetch a suitably sized plank from the bomb peck, and a length of rope from a pile which has been lying there for ages. Within a couple of hours they have made a really superb go kart, and with all the usual strictures about girls not really being up to doing what boys can do obviously being relaxed, the Gang push us up to the top of the hill where Guildford Street meets Lozells, give me the steering rope, put my sister behind me, clinging on for dear life and give us a push, "We'll see you at the bottom!"

At first this is *wonderful*. It is like *flying*. We speed down the hill, the Gang yelling encouragement as they follow in hot pursuit and all the old ladies come to the front door staring in astonishment. I steer my ropes with confidence, gaining speed, soaring past Ruddles, soaring down the street, soaring past the house, where our delighted shrieks bring out my mother, a saucepan in each hand, and Floss, sweeping her front yard – and...

The go kart has a fateful flaw. It has no brakes.

We are screaming now, with no end in sight to our trip, and my mother and Floss are in hot pursuit, closely followed by the Gang. Eventually, as we head towards Summer Lane and its traffic, my mother bangs together the saucepans and yells:

"Steer into the gutter! Steer into the gutter!"

I steer the go kart into the puddles in the gutter, where my sister and I end up sobbing heaps, dresses torn and dirty, mud on our faces, knees and elbows scratched and grazed.

My mother and Floss are *furious*.

"That's the end of the Gang," says my mother ominously as Floss pursues David and Mark back home with her broom, yelling "Wait till your father gets home!"

When Bert does get home, he immediately retires to the outside toilet with the *Daily Mirror* and a packet of Woodbines. Bert *hates* conflict.

The next time we see David and Mark, they are cool.

"We think that you had better play with the other *girls* from now on," they say loftily.

Prayers, tears and pleading are all of no avail and so we are consigned to the great male/female divide, just as the go kart is consigned to the bonfire.

21. High Days, Holidays and Bonfire Nights

There are some festivals in the street which are non events, like Valentine's Day; everyone on the street works too hard to be romantic.

St George's Day also passed without a whimper; all the teachers are *Welsh*. On St David's Day we pipe *Men of Harlech* to Mrs Burton's accompaniment and translation, and Mr Sims is presented with a pot of daffodils.

Hallowe'en is also a non event; the American custom of trick or treating hasn't caught on yet, and nobody can afford to buy something as useless as a pumpkin when you can buy a cabbage to eat instead.

The year starts with New Year's Eve, and my parents always go out for what is called a dinner dance, or a cabaret at somewhere like the King's in West Bromwich or The Talk of the Town in Great Barr. Sometimes this is a works do, but more likely it is with a group of friends, the Atkins, the Bowmans, Claire and Harold Styles or Roy McManus and they hire a charabanc which picks my parents up on Summer Lane. This is due to the introduction of breathalyser tests and seat belts by Barbara Castle ("Worst thing she ever did," mutters my father).

My mother's beehive reaches new heights and she has a glittering array of cocktail frocks, and my father is dressed up in his Burton's the Tailor's suit, and a dazzling white shirt and silk tie from Marks and Spencer's.

We spend the evening with my nan, who puffs away furiously on her fags as we watch Andy Stewart in the White Heather Club. Midnight brings Uncle John, who is tall and dark, first footing through the door with a lump of coal (of which we have plenty, we have two cellars). Then Nan shoos us up to bed, while he waits to escort her back up the entry, after my parents get back in various stages of inebriation. Of course, New Year's Day is not a holiday, so my father still has to get up at half past five, light the fires, put on his overalls and his mac, and pedal off furiously on one of the ramshackle old bikes in the shed to Perry Barr in the wind and the rain. He daren't drive because of the vast amounts of beer he has sunk the night before.

"Of course, there was hardly anyone else there, they were all off sick with hangovers," he reflects gloomily on his return home.

We spend New Year's Day with Mom, watching all the special programmes on the TV. She has saved, in a silver edged napkin, the petits fours from the dinner for us to eat, and she always has an autographed photo from whatever the 'cabaret' was for us to paste into our autograph book. Often they are crooners we have never heard of, but one time it is Ken Dodd, and we love Ken Dodd and the diddymen on the telly.

February brings my birthday, which *always* seems to be on a schoolday. Exciting parcels wrapped up in string and brown paper have been arriving for days; the postman knocks when he arrives with them. My mother stacks them on the sideboard with my cards, and I always get up early on my birthday so I can open all my cards and presents before I go to school. My mother always wraps up as well a little gift for my sister – a jigsaw, a purse – so she doesn't feel left out. One year, one particularly exciting parcel from Aunty Eileen turns out to be a jack in the box!

School is a bit of a trial. As we are such a small school, every child who has a birthday is called out to the front in Assembly; Mr Sims presents you with a birthday card and the whole school sings *Happy Birthday* to Mrs Burton's accompaniment. It is a great ordeal to me; I stand there, clutching my card, crimson with embarrassment.

My mother says we can go to the pictures at the weekend, but we don't have birthday parties with a cake and games as some kids do. It's because of the house of course; it's too small and anyone who came round would have to use the outside toilet. I am very envious of Lynne Atkins, whose parents have moved to a three up two down in Sutton Coldfield, and it has a swing in the back garden! Her birthday is in August, so it is *always* in the school holidays and her mom, my Aunty Barbara, has a real party for her with sandwiches, jellies with thin cream and thick cream, and a pink and white iced cake. I am always cross because I have to eat the sandwiches, which are boring, first. Lynne always has a pretty dress; one year I envy a white organdie affair with red frills.

My mother doesn't feel she can send us with cotton frocks; she has to buy a real party dress which annoys her because by Christmas, when they would next be useful, we may have grown out of them. One August, she takes us resignedly to Littlewood's in Birmingham, where she selects a pale blue nylon party frock, all frills, ribbons and sash, for my sister.

She runs her expert eye over me,

"Something as bit plainer for you," she announces, fingering a plain green A line velveteen.

She is right of course; I don't look right in frills and furbelows. I am small and thin, with straight brown hair and straight features and a serious expression. I don't really look like a child, as my nan says laughingly, I look, really, like a very small adult.

"Mom, please don't buy me that, I want one just like Susannah's only in pink," I beg with tears in my eyes.

Rather dubiously, my mother buys both ("I can take one back").

When my father gets home, Nan and Uncles Bill and John come down, and we proudly parade our new frocks for them. Everyone agrees that my sister looks adorable, but there is a lot of tut tutting over me.

"Doesn't suit her at all," says someone.

Eyes wide, startled, I look around at them all – who said that, and why are they all nodding? I look wildly at my father and run over to him, burying my face against him and sobbing.

"That's enough now," says my nan sharply, but the pink frills go back to the shop and I resign myself to the inevitable.

February is also Pancake Day, and the only day when my mother doesn't make us tea before she goes off to Lucas's. She supplies my father with a large frying pan, eggs, milk, flour and salt and the stricture "Don't make too much mess." My father flips his pancakes with elan, offering us a choice of jam or honey with them.

Pancake Day means the run up to Easter and the holidays. Mr Sims begins reading the Easter story to us at school and Mr Brown, the singing vicar, brings in his guitar to lead us in a rendition of Easter hymns.

There is a green hill far away,
Without a city wall!

Every year we act a play for Easter, and the year I am in Top Class, I am Mary Magdalene in the story of Easter Sunday. I am very proud of my costume, a long skirt and a veil over my head, but very nervous about acting in front of the whole school.

We assemble in the hall as the classes march in one by one and as they are all seated, I step forward with new confidence and begin:

"They have taken away the Lord!"

I have jumped my cue; I was supposed to wait for Mr Tapper, the Top Class teacher to introduce the story. He steps forward, laughing, to send me back to my place and now I am mortified, as when I start properly all the big boys snigger. I decide that I no longer want to be an actress, one of my many chosen careers, I'll be a reporter on a newspaper instead.

Most of the shops are closed on Good Friday, which is a very quiet day, so my mother buys Hot Cross buns the day before. Ranged on the sideboard are our Easter eggs, nearly all Cadbury's of course.

Usually, we don't go away for Easter, although my parents have a week off. They have to save up for the two week summer holiday. But my dad has a friend, Stan Atkins, who works for the BOC; it is his daughter Lynne whose birthday party we go to. Dad loaned Stan some money for a deposit on a house in Sutton Coldfield, and Stan hasn't forgotten this. He has saved up enough money to buy, with a kind of early time share, a caravan in Porthmadog in North Wales, and he asks us to go and spend the Easter week there.

Now that we have the car, this isn't a problem. My father has bought a roof rack to fix the trunk to it, and all five of us are going, squashed into a caravan with the four Atkinses. My dad goes to bed on the afternoon of Good Friday, and gets up at midnight when we set off; there is no motorway in Wales so he wants to avoid the Bank Holiday traffic and arrive at breakfast time. Another bonus of night travel is that me and my sister, propped up in the back with my nan between us, will sleep through the night and maybe, just maybe, I won't be sick (although there are a lot of Co-op carrier bags in the car in case of this).

Our clothing is a bit sturdier than our summer holiday garb, as my mother hears it rains a lot in Wales, so she packs umbrellas, macs and wellies.

I remember little of what must have been an epic journey through the night, as we sleep thorough it, although of course when I do wake up I am instantly sick. My father resignedly disposes of the Co-op sick bags, remarking grimly as he does that there is some corner of a foreign field that is forever Gracie. It's from a poem he learned at school when the only learning aids were memory and the blackboard and he's never forgotten it; my mother can still do the whole of *I wandered lonely as a cloud*.

We wake up just as we get to Beddgelert, on time for breakfast in a greasy spoon café, where we have eggs, bacon and sausages washed down with weak tea in thick white cups, and my father tells us the sad story of Gelert.

My sister and I look at each other, put down our knives and forks, and burst into tears.

My mother is *furious.*

"It's as bad as when they watch *Greyfriars Bobby* or *Lassie Come Home* on the telly!"

The thought of these sad films makes us bawl louder than ever, so my parents bundle us out of the cafe, into the car, and down some very winding, twisty lanes, which turn me green, to Black Rock Sands Holiday Park, Porthmadog. My father has something on his mind. He has heard that some counties in Wales are *dry* on a Sunday; is this one of them?

Nine of us are squashed into one very small caravan, but after a huge cooked breakfast every day, we assemble towels, beachballs, swimming costumes, bottles of White's lemonade, deckchairs, a huge flask of tea and a pile of cheese and tomato sandwiches, and trek straight down to the beach.

My father also has a curious structure on three wooden legs called a windbreaker, which he assembles by sticking it into the sand, and by draping a few towels over it, it also serves as a place where we can modestly get changed into our swimming costumes. He and Uncle Stan take us down to the sea every day, where we are terrified by the extremely large jellyfish.

My mother, Nan and Aunty Barbara lounge in their deckchairs, read the *Daily Mirror* and smoke.

There are no washing or toilet facilities in the caravan – just like home – so after a day on the beach, my mother and Aunty Barbara herd us off to the shower blocks, where the showers with hot running water are a novelty.

There are very few places to eat, so mainly my parents go off and get us fish and chips in the caravan, which we think is a real treat, and at night my parents and Stan and Barbara walk down to Porthmadog to the pub.

Sometimes my mother thinks she should try cooking in the caravan, as fish and chips every night can't be good for us. Porthmadog only houses a Mace, which she doesn't like, so she and Barbara go to the butcher's to buy some lamp chops. They make the mistake of asking for New Zealand lamb chops.

"This is Wales," says the butcher with superb hauteur. "We only have Welsh lamb chops."

It does rain, as my mother predicted, and one exciting morning we wake up to find the caravan surrounded by a deep pool of water. This is terribly exciting for us – we put on our wellies and pick snails out of the puddles – while the grown ups smoke, listen to the radio, read the *Daily Mirror* and play cards.

"Most Brummies have Welsh blood," says my father. "It's like coming home."

May brings the Bank Holiday weekend and a trip to the Lickey Hills to pick the bluebells, and at the end of school term the school trip, which is always to Dudley Zoo, Drayton Manor Park, Trentham Gardens or Alton Towers. My parents send in the weekly payment, sighing as they think of me retching on a coach. On the big day, we are both supplied with a packed lunch, spending money, and in my case a supply of plastic bags. But they don't want me left at school, because that is where the kids who are too poor to go stay.

I always feel that I should bring my mother a present from these days out. One year I bring her a small dog made out of chalk, which crumbles almost instantly, and another year a string of green beads, because that is her favourite colour.

The long summer holidays culminate in the August Bank holiday, and my parents have Monday off. This means a day out in the car, usually at Stourport on Severn or Ross on Wye, or maybe as far as Betwys y Coed. Once or twice we go to Weston Super Mare, or Birmingham on Sea as people call it, although my father worries about being caught in the Bank Holiday traffic. Wherever we go, my parents arrange to meet some of their friends in a pub, and we kids lark about in the children's room with our bottles of Vimto and Smith's Crisps with a blue paper twist of salt in it. But wherever we go, there is a river or the sea; it's such a change as Birmingham is so landlocked. One of my father's friends has saved enough money to buy a very small speedboat which he keeps at Stourport on Severn, and he takes us for trips along the river.

After the long summer holidays, the next big excitement is the Harvest Festival at school. Mr Sims asks everyone in the school to bring in a contribution for parcels for the elderly, although some of the kids themselves come from very poor families. But we always do have a big show of parcels on display at our special assembly, decorated with sheafs of wheat and corn, as together we belt out the Harvest Hymn:

We plough the fields and scatter
The good seed on the land!
But it is fed and watered by God's almighty hand!

We choose a parcel to take to poor Mrs Owen in our back yard, although my mother looks askance on any form of charity.

October brings half term, and although my parents don't get a holiday, they do arrange to take us, along with thousands of other Brummies, up to Blackpool for The Illuminations. This is another epic car journey, done in a day, but it is worth it when we get there. The sandy beach runs for miles and miles, and we get to have a ride on a donkey, just like all the girls in the books I borrow from the library who have their very own ponies, I think, as my donkey canters along the sand.

My father also pays for the five of us to take a journey in a horse and carriage along the front, and this brings us to the hotel where we are having afternoon tea. I have never seen such paper thin slices of bread and butter, arranged prettily on flowery plates, and the sugar for our tea is in lumps, and my mother has to pick them up with little sugar tongs!

This is followed by a trip to the Fun Fair. I am banned from going on anything that goes round and round because of my travel sickness and so I gaze on mournfully as my sister rides a horse on the merry go round. My parents won't take us on the Big Dipper – they say it looks too frightening – but we do go on the Helter Skelter, and meet the White Rabbit in Alice in Wonderland's house. Then Dad and I take on my mum and my sister on the bumper cars, chasing each other round and bumping as hard as we can. But best of all is the Ghost Train, with things that drift across your face, and ghostly chuckles in the dark, but I don't see too much as I am hiding my face against Dad.

Dad loves the amusement arcades with their slot machines, and he has saved up his pennies for a long time. We feed them into machines where we bet on four running horses, into machines where we try and knock down a huge pile of pennies (we never do), into machines where a long claw descends and you try and pick up something from an exciting array of prizes and into one armed bandits, where you need three oranges to line up to win a prize.

After a fish and chip supper and a toffee apple or a candy floss for me and my sister, it's time to make our way home, with a slow drive down the front where The Illuminations stretch the length of the Golden Mile and we hang out of the windows to look at them.

Bonfire Night is the next big event. Every yard has a bonfire and everyone saves up discarded furniture, old planks, anything really to burn on the bonfire, so you can make sure you have the biggest bonfire on the street! Some even wheel out old pianos up the entry and into the yard, which makes my nan cross.

"My mother – your great grandmother – had a piano, and in the evenings and at Christmas, we'd gather round it and sing while she played. You made your own entertainment, not just turn on the radio or telly," she remarks shortly, although Nan *loves* the TV and radio.

David and Mark make a guy out of Bert's old clothes, station it on the pavement, put Bert's flat cap upside down, and every time someone walks past, beg:

"A penny for the guy?"

My father goes off to the House That Jack Built, and buys a vast array of fireworks: sparklers, Catherine Wheels, jumping jacks, rockets, and whizzbangs.

There is an old lady who lives halfway up Geach Street on the way to our school; her door is split in two, and she opens the top half, sets out a tray, and sells toffee apples for a penny each. My mother walks up to buy some for everyone in the yard.

On the actual night, David and Mark lug their guy up the entry and sling it onto the bonfire, which makes me and my sister cry again and hide our eyes. My father sloshes around a bit of petrol and applies a match, and up goes our bonfire in flames, although my sister and I think it is so sad for the guy.

My father and Bert and Mr Docker, with stern warnings to the rest of us to keep back, set off a superb display of fireworks, although we are allowed to hold our sparklers and write our name in the air.

It's all a bit sad when it is over, but then the best festival of all is still to come.

22. Have yourself a
Merry Little Christmas

Christmas doesn't start as early then as it does now. The first signs are when my mother's Autumn/Winter Burlington's Catalogue arrives in September. My sister and I love looking at the toys and books in the Christmas section and the big Christmas hampers which we never have.

My mother checks that our present party dresses are suitable for Christmas; otherwise it's off to Lewis's or Littlewood's for new ones.

Come December, the Christmas decorations go up at school, including a huge, glittering Christmas tree in the hall. In Assembly we begin to sing the Advent hymns:

Hills of the north, rejoice!
O come O come Emmanuel,
Redeem thy captive Israel!

Casting begins for the Nativity play; in Mrs Burton's year, perhaps due to her tutoring in reading aloud clearly, I am at last chosen to be the Virgin Mary.

"About time too," says my grandmother.

My sister is to be both the Innkeeper's daughter and a shepherd with a teatowel on her head (we are such a small school that we are non gender discriminatory). After Assembly we stay on in the hall for rehearsal with Mrs Burton and Mr Tapper, and I get fitted for my costume, made by Mrs Wardell; a long blue dress with a white veil over my head, made out of a pillowcase.

The rest of the school practise the Christmas carols we sing at the play and in Assembly every morning; all the old favourites learnt off by heart: *Hark! The herald angels sing, Away in a Manger, Little Donkey, The Holly and the Ivy, O come all Ye Faithful, O little Town of Bethlehem,* and *Once in Royal David's City.* As we have no song sheets or hymn books, all of these have to be learnt off by heart.

At home my father, after much grumbling, spends hours putting up paper chains bought from the House That Jack Built. We don't have enough room for a real tree but my mother puts our little green one in the corner next to the television and decorates it with tinsel, glittering Christmas tree balls, and my particular favourites, little angels in pink dresses and with golden wings. My sister and I give these angels names and make up stories about them.

Two weeks before Christmas, my mother buys the (very thick) *Radio Times* and *TV Times* so she can mark up her favourite programmes and she orders the turkey, the pork crackling and the sausages and bacon from the butcher's. She has been saving all year with their Christmas Club so much of it is paid for already.

At school, the singing vicar comes in every Friday to tell us the Christmas story. Mr Sims has, every year, with variations, his own version of *A Christmas Carol*. He stands in front of us in his neat black suit, rubbing his hands together.

"Well once upon a time, there was a miser called *Scrooge*. A miser, children, is someone who is very mean with his money."

Someone raises their hand.

"Where did he live, sir?" All the teachers are sir and miss.

"Well, Scrooge lived in Birmingham, but he wasn't a Brummie, he was from the Black Country. That's why he was so mean." Mr Sims permits himself a chuckle at his own joke as we gaze back blankly and the teachers snigger.

All the same, I love the story and tell my mum about it. She comes up trumps as usual; a copy of Charles Dickens' *Christmas Stories* from the House That Jack Built, the universal provider, with a queer picture on the front of a white faced Scrooge. I find the illustrations quite frightening, but I love the story, although I don't like the other stories in it, *The Chimes* and *The Cricket on the Hearth*.

The Nativity play takes place in the last week of school right after Assembly, and my mum and my nan watch my sister piping "No room at the Inn!" with tears in their eyes. Afterwards there is tea and mince pies for parents and teachers.

Both Lucas's and Tucker Fasteners throw grand Christmas parties for their employees' children. The men work for weeks setting up the decorations and the women prepare to be aunties. We children are dressed up to the nines, girls in frilly frocks and the boys in shorts and shirts with a dicky bow. These parties always involve sumptuous teas of sandwiches, jellies, ice cream and cake. Tucker's is in the canteen and we play party games with balloons, but actually, although we never say so, we much prefer Lucas's where you get a film show of Disney cartoons and a really splendid present; one year I get a tennis racket and six balls!

My mother takes us to see Father Christmas, usually at Lewis's, Birmingham, or maybe the co-op, where he awaits us in a glistening grotto, but this year, it is even better as it is a boat ride up the Congo at the Co-op, and the boat *really moves from side to side*. Afterwards, my mother takes us to hear the Salvation Army playing Christmas carols outside Rackham's and the snowflakes glisten on their dark uniforms. Every street, New Street, Corporation Street, Colmore Row, glitters with lights and the Christmas tree in Victoria Square is a present from the people of Norway, to thank the people of Birmingham for what we suffered during the war.

Sometimes, not every year, it snows and the street is transformed. The bomb peck becomes an exciting Alpine landscape and every puddle is frozen. My mother sends us out in scarves, wellingtons, coats, hats and gloves to build snowmen and have snowball fights. But we don't have a sledge; what is the point? Birmingham is as flat as a pancake. We walk to school as usual in the snow and sit in our coats if it is cold (school *never* closes).

By the last week of school, all the children are fit to burst with excitement, and the teachers give up trying to teach us. We make Christmas cards for them in art on thick card, illustrated by ourselves with our watercolour palettes and with thick sprinklings of glitter. On the last day, Friday, we are allowed to finish at lunchtime, so those of us who are not on school dinners run out joyously.

My mother finished at Lucas's the night before and she went there this morning to get her pay packet which contains a Christmas bonus. She and my grandmother have already been to the Co-op, staggering back with shopping trollies of sprouts, cabbage, carrots and green peas; in the afternoon it's off to the baker's for the Christmas pudding, the mince pies and the Christmas cake. The milkman has left us bread and orange juice and eggs; every shop in Birmingham is about to close down for two whole days.

My father also finishes at lunchtime with a bonus and arrives home in tearing high spirits. He has done the important shopping in his view; as he is the driver, he stopped at the off licence for the heavy stuff and he has cans of Ansells and Watney's for himself, and Babychams and Waarninks Advocaat for snowballs and big bottles of White's or Cader Idris lemonade for us. Another stop at Ruddles for two big boxes of Cadbury's Roses and Quality Street, which we love because of the pretty lady and the gallant soldier on the tin. My mother and nan get a box of Weekend candies, which makes us jealous as they are such pretty colours. We just have a tin of Blue Bird toffees with the Blue Boy on the lid, and crystallized oranges and lemon jellies in a round box.

Christmas Eve is bath night in the tin bath in front of the fire. There is usually a *Top of the Pops Special* on the telly and carol singers from the street come around. But my sister and I are too excited to concentrate on anything. We have asked for roller skates this year, and Father Christmas usually brings us what we want! We have elaborate plans to stay awake in shifts *all night* waiting for Father Christmas. We have already been to see him at the Co-op, and this year it wasn't a fairy grotto, it was an exciting trip up the Congo in a boat.

"Leave Santa a glass of brandy, it's cold outside," says my father with a wink; we insist also on a mince pie (he's a busy man) and a carrot for Rudolf!

Of course, despite our best intentions, we fall asleep almost immediately, and the next minute, my mother is standing on the landing in her dressing gown, carrying a tray with the teapot and four cups, and calling:

"Merry Christmas Gracie! Merry Christmas bab! Santa has been!"

We leap out of bed and put on our dressing gowns and slippers and run down to their room. Dad is lying in bed in his pyjamas beaming and the floor is full of a mass of excitingly wrapped presents!

We leave Mom and Dad's till last. All the rest are from the family. Aunty Eileen always gives me a book token to spend at the Midland Educational. There is a handbag or a purse from my nan and dolls, teddies and games from uncles and aunties. There is a Cadbury's Selection Box for each of us, and tins of Bluebird Toffee. Last of all, we unwrap Mum and Dad's present with squeals of joy; roller skates with rubber wheels and laces across the front, and for once we are really glad it isn't snowing!

In other years, presents might be a dolls' house, carpeted and curtained by my father, or a farmyard with a set of animals and people. One Christmas we have a real Hornby electric train set; this is of course, the present my dad always wanted when he was a child and never got. He lays it carefully on the tiny living room floor and is extremely cross when we tie people from the farmyard set onto the line, or play at the Great Train Robbery.

Mom and Dad lie in bed smoking and watching us and drinking tea; but they have to get up and cook a full breakfast of sausages, fried bread, bacon and eggs. Then Dad goes up to the shed to fetch the turkey; it needs to go into the oven straight away and they've got all the vegetables to do, gravy to make from the vegetable water and the pudding to boil.

My mother supervises our washing, dresses us up in our best, brushes my hair till it gleams and ties up my sister's blonde ponytail with a red and gold ribbon.

"On the sofa," she says. "You can't go out dressed like that."

Actually we don't mind because the telly is actually on all day today. We watch a Christmas Carol service, and then there is one in Welsh, but we hear the teachers speaking Welsh at school so we don't mind that. There's always a programme where Leslie Crowther and Peter Glaze, who we love from *Crackerjack*, visit kids in hospital, and by the time this is over, Dad is setting up the green baize card table with a special Christmas tablecloth and napkins, and carving the turkey.

Over plates piled high, my father raises his Watney's.

"Merry Christmas everyone!"

Dinner has to be over by 3 pm so we can watch the Queen; Mom boils the kettle for a mountain of washing up and generally Mom and Dad then fall asleep while we watch *Disney Time* and Billy Smart's Circus.

At six o'clock, my parents wake up as Nan, Floss, Bert, David and Mark come in to wish us a Merry Christmas. Uncle John has gone out on the town with his mates, so there are nine of us squashed into a tiny living room, with us kids on our parents' laps.

My mother makes turkey and chicken sandwiches, and brings out the Christmas cakes and a huge shivering jelly with thin or thick cream, and packets of Smith's Crisps with the little blue salt packet. There is Mackeson's for Bert, and Babycham and snowballs for the ladies. Nan passes around cigarettes and soon the air is thick with smoke. Bert rolls his own. He has smoked 80 a day since he was 14 and will live to be 90.

Sometimes we watch what is on the telly – maybe a pantomime or *Christmas Night with the Stars* – but usually my dad loads six of his singles onto the drop down record player and we all have a dance to the hits of the year.

At midnight, my sister and I look at each other in consternation as we realise that it is all over for another year.

"Never mind," says my mother. "It's Boxing Day tomorrow and you can wrap up warm and go out and play all day on your roller skates."

Guildford Street in the 1960s.

Mom, 1948 in 2/37 Guildford Street.

My sister in her pram, on our street, 1959.

Mom and Dad on their Wedding Day, 19th December 1953. Dad's suede shoes cost 10/6d.

Uncle Albert and Auntie Mary's Engagement photo.

Sun Valley, Paignton, 1960.

Mom in the back yard.

My grandmother, 1928; she had just had her hair bobbed. Studio photo by Dyche.

Nan, Mom and Uncle Bill, 1939.

Uncle Bill and Auntie Margaret's Wedding Day.

Author (front) at Lucas's Christmas Party, 1960s.

My sister at Lucas's Christmas Party, 1960s.

Lucas's Christmas Party, 1965.

B3 Assembly Line, Lucas's. Mom front row, second from left.

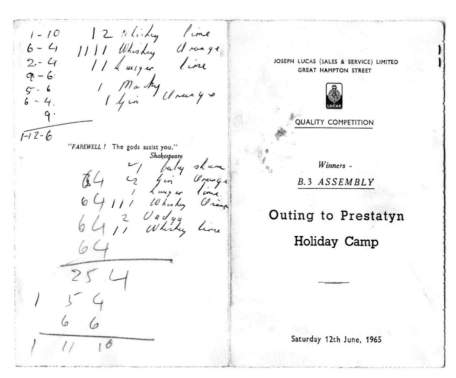

JOSEPH LUCAS (SALES & SERVICE) LIMITED
GREAT HAMPTON STREET

QUALITY COMPETITION

Winners -

B.3 ASSEMBLY

Outing to Prestatyn
Holiday Camp

Saturday 12th June, 1965

B3 Assembly, Lucas, outing to Prestatyn Holiday Camp, 12th June, 1965.

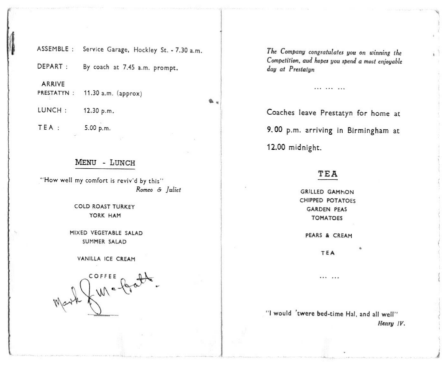

ASSEMBLE :   Service Garage, Hockley St. - 7.30 a.m.

DEPART :   By coach at 7.45 a.m. prompt.

ARRIVE
PRESTATYN : 11.30 a.m. (approx)

LUNCH :   12.30 p.m.

TEA :   5.00 p.m.

MENU - LUNCH

"How well my comfort is reviv'd by this"
                        Romeo & Juliet

COLD ROAST TURKEY
YORK HAM

MIXED VEGETABLE SALAD
SUMMER SALAD

VANILLA ICE CREAM

COFFEE

The Company congratulates you on winning the Competition, and hopes you spend a most enjoyable day at Prestatyn

... ...

Coaches leave Prestatyn for home at 9.00 p.m. arriving in Birmingham at 12.00 midnight.

TEA

GRILLED GAMMON
CHIPPED POTATOES
GARDEN PEAS
TOMATOES

PEARS & CREAM

TEA

... ...

"I would 'twere bed-time Hal, and all well"
                        Henry IV.

Inside of the Prestatyn Holiday Camp programme showing outing details.

William Cowper Junior and Infant School, 1960s.

School photo, 1966.

William Cowper is demolished, 1972.

The house on the day we left.

First day in the new house, June 1968.

23. Parks and Recreation/Sports and Leisure/Out and About

My mother cannot see that we need anywhere else to play. We have a splendid back yard with a collection of ramshackle sheds and we have the bomb peck. The street itself is a playground; hardly any cars pass down in and the boys play footie in the road.

There's no doubt, however, that Birmingham has some splendid parks. We are a civic Victorian city, built on the backs of the industrial revolution, and we have fine parks, splendid recreation halls, gin palaces which look like stately homes, and ornate cinemas; so many, alas, to go within the next generation. The council gave them to us; the council will take them away.

"Nobody cares about working-class heritage," says my dad.

The nearest park to us is the Tower Hill one on Tower Street, by the Birmingham Settlement; it is so close that we can walk there with David and Mark. There isn't much grass, but like all of our parks it has lovely flower beds, very important to those who don't have gardens. What we like is the little playground. It has a slide and swings and a roundabout which you can perch on while you spin it round with your foot, but the other kids will grab it and spin it faster and faster.

This park is guarded, as they all are then, by a very fierce parkie. He lives in a little shed by the gate and he chases the lads when they send the swings over the tops of their stands and tangle the chains up.

What we long for is water. Birmingham is as landlocked as you get. Hockley Brook is underground; David and Mark tell us it is what you can hear gurgling away when you are in the outside toilet and if you fall down the hole, you'll be swept away. The River Tame is up by Witton Cemetery in the middle of an industrial estate.

Of course we have miles and miles of (now neglected) canals, all built by the navvies to bring in goods to Birmingham. But now everyone uses lorries, so there are miles and miles of them, unused, neglected and surrounded by crumbling red brick warehouses. More miles of canal than Venice, says my father, and takes us on a canal boat trip from the Gas Street Basin. But we don't get too far as the propeller keeps silting up with all the waste and dead animals people throw into the canal.

My sister and I are so desperate for a stream, a river, a pond or a lake that we dig a hole in the dirt in the backyard and pour water into it, but of course it goes straight through. My nan feels sorry for us and gives us an old jelly mould to fit into it and now we have a pond.

My nan also takes us to Burbury Street Park one hot, sunny afternoon, as there is a paddling pool there. We tuck our frocks up into our knickers and have a great time paddling. It's so hot that we soon get thirsty and my nan takes us over to a small newsagent's on the corner. There is an old lady in there, with a flowery pinny and her grey hair in a bun. She pours us all a glass of raspberryade from a bottle, which we drink there and then; she has a glass herself as Nan pays her, a penny a glass and says she will drink the rest for her tea.

Aston Park is also very close to us and Dad takes us up there on a Saturday to see Aston Hall. It is Birmingham's very own stately home, dating right back to the 1600s, and built in a mellow red brick. The founder was Sir Thomas Holte, so that's why everything is called Holte round here. Aston Hall is free for kids and only sixpence for adults and you get to see all of the hall. The long gallery has a huge portrait of Sir Thomas and his eyes follow you wherever you go. He was the Bad Baronet, says my dad, and the security attendant tells us some tales of Sir Thomas.

"Yes, he was a bit of a bad lad. He took his cook's meat cleaver and cut his head in half because he didn't like his dinner .... His poor daughter, she wouldn't marry the man he wanted her to marry, so he locked her up in the attics and she starved to death ... So they say the hall is haunted ...."

This is quite thrilling as is the guide's assertion that there *might* be a secret passage between the hall and Aston Parish church, where the Holtes are buried and so many of our family were christened, and the family *might* have hidden the family jewels there during the Civil War. Exploring for secret passages becomes our new game.

Aston Park, like all of our parks, has wonderful flower beds, but we are more thrilled by the sight of Villa Park, in all its red brick glory, just behind it. Everybody in the family supports the Villa. Everyone in the street, indeed in Aston, supports The Villa. It is part of *who we are.*

Although it is two bus rides away, my nan likes to take us to Cannon Hill Park in Edgbaston every spring for the Tulip Festival, because she loves tulips. On the bus, she tells us the story of Sir Frank Price, the founder.

"Well, he was just ordinary, like us, from Hockley, but he got to be on the council and he thought the parks were for all of us. He ordered all the tulips from Holland and had them planted in Cannon Hill Park, and he said there was to be a Dutch Festival for us all to enjoy."

The festival is indeed splendid, with smiling girls in Dutch costumes handing out buttonholes, displays of clog and lace making, a balloon floating overhead, and entertainers everywhere. My nan enjoys the bandstand; we sit on little chairs in the sunshine, listening to *Marche Militaire* and *Colonel Bogie.* The park itself is a wonder; 9,000 tulips bloom, the River Rea runs through it, and there are lakes with paddle boats. The whole day is capped off with a splendid fireworks display.

A bus ride away are what we call the two Perry parks; Perry Hall and Perry Park in Perry Barr, and they are right opposite each other. My nan likes Perry Hall because it has a tea room and boating moat where we can hire paddle boats. She tells us that she can remember Perry Hall which used to stand there.

"Well, the council had the choice of knocking down Perry Hall or Aston Hall and they chose Perry Hall."

We love the moat and the paddle, boats and the bit in the middle with its little bridges. My nan sits on the bench in the sun, watching us and reading the *Mail*; she takes us into the tiny tea room where she has a cup of tea from the big urn and we have blackcurrant squash and everyone gets a cream bun.

We four children love Perry Park, although the grown ups think it is boring. It has a rather nondescript playground, no tea room, and no flower beds. But it has a very exciting river, which is really the Perry Reservoir, running right through it, and we can get right next to it. Outside the gate there is a little shop on the corner, and they sell fishing nets, so armed with these and a jam jar we spend exciting summer afternoons paddling and catching newts.

"Don't fall in for God's sake," says my mother resignedly.

Sometimes on a Sunday in is the holidays my father takes us in the car to Sutton Park in Sutton Coldfield, which is *huge,* and we meet the Atkins family there. You can walk for hours in forest and woodland, but what we like best are the seven lakes, and the best of all is Keepers' Pool because it is an open air swimming pool and I do love to swim!

Nobody in the family can swim except Dad and he learnt in the Marines. He does an old fashioned breast stroke. Maybe it is because Birmingham is full of derelict canals, but the City Council thinks that all the children of landlocked Birmingham should be able to swim and from school we go off once a week on a Corporation bus to Nechells Swimming Baths, where we splash about using little white plastic floats as we work for our Swimming badges.

Actually, me and my sister can already swim. Dad has been taking us since we were three every Tuesday night to Kingstanding Baths. We go here because there is a little pool for us. We love our swimming costumes but we hate the plastic caps Mom makes us wear, because she won't have us coming home in winter with dripping hair. We have enough colds already.

We love swimming; we love the changing rooms and the footbath you have to pass through to get to the pool (my mother utters dire warnings of warts and veruccas). Dad patiently teaches us the front crawl (he doesn't think much of the breast stroke he can do), dressed in the baggy blue trunks he has had since his National Service Days. He says when we can do a length, we can go into the exciting Big Pool where he swims and it has a diving board!

Mom lets Dad take us to the park, the library and the swimming pool. She thinks we are happy enough as we are, and she isn't particularly sociable, and she has very little free time but she does make the occasional effort to enrol us in groups where she doesn't have to stay (she is too busy).

There is a Girls' Life Brigade Group at the Baptist church at Six Ways, and my mother was a member in the Thirties, so she takes us up there. We spend a lot of time raiding a dressing up box to do a play. It doesn't last as long as the Brownies, which we join when we are seven. The Brownies meet at the Birmingham Settlement on Tower Street, a big draughty hall set up in 1899 to serve the poorest communities in Birmingham. It has a savings bank, a clinic for babies, a library, a Citizens' Advice Bureau and lots of sports clubs; David and Mark play cricket and football there. Brownies meets in the hall on a Tuesday night, and we have a Brown Owl who is dark and middle-aged with horn rimmed glasses, and Tawny Owl who is older and white haired.

My mother has to draw money out of the Post Office Savings Bank to buy us the uniform; a brown overall with a tie, and the Golden Man, our membership badge, which Dad polishes with Brasso every week.

Dressed in our brand new uniforms, we stand in front of Brown Owl and devoutly recite the Brownie vow:

I promise to do my best
To do my duty to God and the Queen ...

I am always a bit distracted by the fact that the library is also situated in the hall where we meet, although the books look grown up and boring. However, we begin by dividing into Sixes and dancing round the Toadstool at the centre of the Circle, as we sing our song:

Here we come the laughing Gnomes,
Helping mothers in our homes!

We're the Fairies, glad and gay
Helping mothers every day!

Here we come the jolly Pixies
Helping people out of fixes!

As well as games, songs, and stories, we work every week for a badge. It's a proud day when you get your Washing up Badge in the Settlement kitchen (although it won't help at home as we don't have running hot water and have to boil the kettle).

Then you get a little cloth badge which Mom sews onto our sleeves. At New Year, we hand over our pocket money for a small red Brownie diary, in which we can write all about our badges. But I love the photos in it of Brownies all over the world.

My sister and I go every week and we reach the dizzying heights of becoming Sixers, or having our very own groups; I am Sixer of the Gnomes, and my sister is Sixer of the Fairies.

Mom is waiting outside with the other mothers as we rush forward to tell her the wonderful news.

"Mom! Mom! I'm Sixer of the Gnomes and Susannah has got the Fairies!"

Before Mom can express appropriate delight, one of the other mothers laughs as she looks at me, small, thin and plain and serious, and Susannah, tiny and dainty with big blue eyes and blonde curls.

"Sounds just right ... one looks like a gnome and the other like a fairy!"

I know what gnomes and fairies look like; they are in my Enid Blyton books. The gnomes are always ugly and bad. I stop, eyes wide, all the breath gone out of me, just like being hit in the tummy, all my joy gone.

On the way home, my mother tries to console me, but it's just one of those moments when the casual cruelty of grown ups destroys the world of the child.

There is a church on the corner of Summer Lane and Geach Street called the Church of Christ. We are Church of England (nominally, because we never go, but it's where everyone is baptised, married and buried). But Birmingham, the dissenting city, is full of churches: Quakers, Unitarians, Baptist, Salvation Army, Methodist.

The Sunday School superintendent comes into assembly and shows us a most beautiful picture book, the Sleeping Beauty, with a lovely Good Fairy on the front, dressed in a sparkling white robe and with glittering wings.

"This is a good attendance prize," she tells us. "It will be given to the child who comes to Sunday School every week between now and Christmas."

I want that book more than I have ever wanted anything. I run home with Susannah in tow.

"Mom, Mom, I need to go to Sunday School in Geach Street every week and I can win a prize!"

My mother agrees with some misgivings as this will mean getting up earlier on Sundays for the next ten weeks in order to have our full cooked breakfast before we go to Sunday School.

On Sundays, then, for the next ten weeks, we trip hand in hand down Geach Street to the Church. Nobody is around, as the street sleeps off Saturday night, and we don't know any of the kids at Sunday School. We listen to stories about Moses in the bulrushes, King David, and a rather exciting story about Cain and Abel, and we colour in little pictures. Susannah is a bit cross about having to get up so early. She would rather stay at home and play with her toys.

On the Sunday before Christmas, we all assemble in front of the superintendent, who smilingly holds up the book. I have been every week and I am sure I am going to win the prize!

"And the winner is ... Terry!"

I have another hit in the tummy moment as Terry, who hasn't been every week, ambles forward, grinning, to claim his prize.

I spring up, grab Susannah's hand and rush home and pour the story, sobbing to my mother.

Usually my mother thinks we need to be a bit more stoic, but she has, after all, sacrificed her Sunday morning lie in for ten weeks for me to win this prize. She puts on her best coat with its coney fur collar to go down to Sunday School.

The superintendent is apologetic but firm.

"Well, you see, we give it to the poorer children, in order to encourage them, and we know Grace has a lot of books and reads already, she's so good at it."

My mother is unimpressed by this early expression of positive discrimination; it just means problems for her.

"No more Sunday School," she remarks grimly, and she gets me my own copy of the *Sleeping Beauty* from the ever obliging House That Jack Built; it's even better than the prize, because Sleeping Beauty has a lovely pink dress.

24. Diversity

My world is that of the white working-classes and the extended family, but Birmingham has been a multicultural city long before the term was invented by trendy liberals. On the whole, we co-exist in perfect peace and harmony.

The largest ethnic group is the Irish, who have been pouring into Birmingham for two hundred years in quest of work. There aren't any Irish children at school because they all go to St Theresa's RC, and there aren't many living round by us because the big Irish quarter is Digbeth and Deritend. But most of my parents' Irish friends live in Great Barr, clustered around the Catholic Church.

"The Catholics really *get* something from their religion," reflects my mother.

"The Irish built Birmingham," says my father; he doesn't mean just the navvies but the self-made men who founded the great construction companies.

My father has no time for the idle on our street who spout the line that the Irish "take our jobs and our housing". Anyone can get a job in Birmingham who is prepared to work hard and study. He himself studies one night a week at Brooklyn Technical College and he has signed up for the Open University correspondence course. Huge packs arrive for him in the post, and he gets up even earlier to listen to the University of the Air on the radio. All this is paid for by the Trade Union and is on top of his forty hours a week job.

As well as all this, my father has a Vernon's pools round on Friday night, after tea; this is to go into the Post Office for our holidays. Actually he quite likes it although he doesn't do the Pools himself: football can never be predicted, he tells us. We like it because he brings us fish and chips after from the Greek's (all fish and chip shops are called Greek, even if they are not). In any case, he goes out with his mate Taff (real name Alf), who is Welsh but has the thickest Black Country accent you have ever heard.

Taff works on the roads, supervising a gang of Poles, and every Friday he comes in and says to my dad:

"Boody 'ard workers, the Poles. Bloody 'ard workers!"

The Poles are those who came over to fight in World War Two and stayed on after; my Great Uncle Bert, who was in the wartime RAF (as a chef), tells me tales of the Free Polish Air Squadron who shot down more of the Luftwaffe than anyone else.

Our Italian community is on the whole descended from the Italian prisoners of war who spent much of the war in a prisoner of war camp in Hockley; my mother remembers them being marched to work in the mornings, blowing kisses at the Birmingham girls.

"They were so handsome," she sighs.

There are some Italian girls at school, the Santini sisters; they are waiting for a place at the Roman Catholic school. Very beautiful they are, says my mother, with their black hair, olive skin and big dark eyes. Their father is married to an Englishwoman and he has an ice cream van of his very own. We can't actually think of a better job for your dad to have. We love to hear the bells of the ice cream van sounding outside on the street and with our pennies, we rush out to buy an ice lolly or a cone with a Cadbury's 99 flake. Luigi knows I am friends with his girls and he always puts raspberry sauce on my cone as he knows I like it.

He gets expansive with my dad one parents' evening.

"Well you see, I was made to join the Fascist party in the thirties, and I didn't like it. My heart just wasn't in being a young fascist," he reflects.

He made his mind up quite early to be captured and spent a lot of the war wandering Italy, looking for the British or the Canadians.

"My English was not good then, but I learnt two phrases: I surrender, and Can I have a cup of tea please?" He thinks this will endear him to his eventual British captors, as indeed it does.

There is a black girl also at school; her name is Blanche, and she doesn't have many friends. I want to be friends with her – I admire the cherry red ribbons in her curly black hair – but I am a bit frightened of her, as she is so confident and I am so shy.

She tells me that she is not there for long, her parents are waiting for a council house on the outskirts of Birmingham, and one day she doesn't come to school any more and that's that.

There aren't any Asian children at school, but some Asian shopkeepers are beginning to appear on the Lozells Rd.

One bright Saturday morning, my nan asks me to go with her to the Lozells Rd as she wants to buy a jumper she has seen in the window of a shop there. I love going out with my nan, so I walk happily up Guildford St with her to the Lozells Rd, where the church is where my grandparents married. My nan is neat in her coat and hat and she has a paste brooch pinned onto her collar.

When we get to the shop she stops and gives me a stern look.

"This shop is now being run by a young Indian man. I don't want you staring at him. It would be rude."

This sounds very exciting and glamorous to me, as we have got a book on India at home that my Great Uncle Fred gave Mom; he was based there during the war, and she has also got a tiny pair of slippers encrusted with gems. So I think of turbans, of saris, of flowing hair and beards.

I am to be disappointed as the young man is immaculately dressed in a dark suit, a tie and a dazzling white shirt, and his black hair is neatly cut and parted. He has a soft voice, a lilting accent and his English is perfect. He and my nan are exquisitely polite as he lifts from the window the stand with the top that has caught her eye, pale gold, short sleeved, and with two buttons on the neck.

I am so keen to get a closer view of him that I lean over the counter and knock the stand; my nan glares, he apologises and Nan glares and says, no it's her fault!

The blouse being satisfactory at 19/11d, he wraps it in soft tissue, and ushers us to the door, opening it for us with a little half bow.

"That was a very nice, polite young man," says my nan outside.

She pauses and adds:

"Some *English* boys could learn a lesson from him."

"The white working-classes, they're by far the worse for prejudice," says my father.

He talks a lot like this since he started the Open University. My mother is telling him about an incident that happened earlier that day and his usually jovial face looks worried.

There is a girl on our street called Joanna and she has got a baby, Michelle, one of the names from other cultures now appearing on our street – Ingrid, Astrid, Yvonne, Tanya – as though the street is looking outwards for the first time. Joanna isn't married to Michelle's father, which is shocking enough, but Michelle's father is what people call coloured. His name is Charlie and he has dazzling white teeth which split his face in half when he smiles, which is often.

Charlie tells my dad that his father came over from Jamaica, in a big boat called the *Windrush*, for a better life. I don't know about that, but Charlie works as a painter and decorator. He goes off in the morning in his white overalls, with his paints and brushes.

Joanna takes Michelle for walks down the street in her pram, and some of the men and women come to their doors and shout things at her.

My nan is interested because Jo's parents are her cousins, Ray and Thelma. When Jo and Charlie got together, both of their families rejected them; that's why they haven't got married, because no-one would come to the wedding. Jo tells Nan that when she got pregnant, Ray and Thelma threw her out, and Charlie's family wouldn't take her in, so she had to go to a home for unmarried mothers to give birth; then he got a council house, but she is there alone all day while he is at work.

One day she walks past her house with the pram and some of the big boys start throwing stones at her.

My nan is having a cup of tea with my mom and they rush out.

"You stop that now!" yells my nan; she is only five foot two and six stone but she is frightened of no-one. She turns on the boys. "Some of you lot have got mums who are down the pub every night and your idle dads are on the dole!"

They bring Jo in, comfort her, give her a cup of tea; she says between sobs that she doesn't know what to do, that Charlie wants to go back to Jamaica, or maybe even Australia, but she doesn't want to go on such a long journey.

My sister and I are looking after Michelle, who is a beautiful baby with light, coffee coloured skin, huge brown eyes and reddish black hair.

"And I don't know what will happen when the bab starts school, if I can even get her into a school, that is."

My nan promises to go and speak to Ray and Thelma later that day.

My sister and I spend the afternoon making up bouquets to take to the elderly on the street. We have had a talk at school from the Vicar about being kind to those who are old and lonely. Fired with enthusiasm, we decide to take them flowers, by which we mean wildflowers, as we haven't got any money, and there aren't any gardens in the street, so we pick the little white flowers growing in the privet, and tie them up with cotton with a few grass seeds and buttercups and daisies which grow between the cracks in the pavement or wild on the bomb peck.

We start off with Harry and Violet, who live a few doors down in a one down two up, like us. I used to think they are married, but my mom says no, they are brother and sister. They both work in local factories, and sometimes we see them out walking arm in arm; Violet in a hat and coat like my nan, and Harry a small man in a neat overcoat, raising his peaked cap to us.

Harry isn't in, but Violet is thrilled with my bouquet. She asks me in and shows me her garden which is long and overgrown like Mrs Owen's, but she has got a pet rabbit in a hutch.

She gives me a few coppers for my bouquet, and even better, a toy she has made herself out of stuffing; a queer looking animal with no ears and brown boot buttons for eyes, but I love her instantly and say I will call her Violet. I run home clutching Violet and my pennies in my hot hand and show them to my mom, but she is *furious*.

"You should never take money from people! Take it back now!" she orders.

Tears fill my eyes and my dad looks uncomfortable but I run back. I daren't ring the doorbell so I leave the pennies on Violet's well scrubbed front doorstep.

When I get back, the atmosphere is calmer. My nan has popped in in her coat and hat; she is off to Ray and Thelma's. My mom is always quieter when nan is around.

"I always wonder," says Mom, "why Violet never married. She's a good looking woman."

"We all know why Harry didn't marry!" interjects my dad, and he and my mom laugh. I don't know why.

"I've known Violet all my life," says my nan. "We were born in the same year, 1908."

She sits on the sofa, still in hat and coat, absentmindedly stirring her tea.

"Violet was one of a big family – she was the eldest – five girls and Harry, and a boy who died, there was.

Vi's mother, Jenny, worked in a factory and she met her husband there. Ted they called him. They had a house on the street – the one Vi lives in now. Two grown ups and six kids in two bedrooms.

Well, Jenny, she had a friend who worked in the factory with her. Nell was her name. She was an orphan and working to keep herself since she was twelve. Quiet girl.

Well, she got pregnant by a man who dumped her. The boarding house, they threw her out onto the street and she lost her job straightaway. It was her old friend Jenny who took her in. She had a little boy, George in 1911, the same year Jenny had a boy, the one who died, so I think Jenny saw it almost as her own. She had Harry two years later.

Nell did marry in the end, a bloke named Fred who knocked her around, and he died of drink. Knocked George around too.

Ted died in the first year of the war, in the trenches, and Jenny had to manage six kids on her own. Vi left school when she was twelve and went to work. She helped with the kids as well. And she said to me, 'Else, I'm not ever getting married and having kids, 'cos all I've ever done is work and look after kids, and if I've got to work till I'm sixty, I'm not looking after kids as well.'

Then Jenny got sick – it was the TB. Nothing to be done. Died in 1920.

It was Nell who helped Vi look after the kids then – always remembered what Jenny had done for her.

All the other girls, they got married young and left home, but Vi, she stayed at the house and Harry with her. George used to go round to the house a lot, especially when his mom died and he was living in the Rowton Houses. Harry was his best friend. They went everywhere together.

People used to say that they were just like an old married couple. Devoted. There were some used to throw stones at them and call them names.

Then the war came and they joined up straightaway. Joined the same regiment. Then George was shot dead in Belgium in front of Harry's eyes.

I don't know how they did it, but Harry got him back to Birmingham and the family paid for a big funeral at Witton. They remembered what Nell had done for them, you see. I can still see the hearse going down the street, with six black horses with feathers on their heads. They put him in with his mum and paid for a fancy big gravestone."

"Well," she sighs, "after the war, Harry came back and he moved in with Vi, and there he stayed. Got a job at Vi's place. Never took up with anyone else. You have to be careful" – she slides her eyes around to me – "the law, you know."

"It's not illegal now," interjects my dad.

"Too late for the likes of Harry and George," responds my nan.

She pauses.

"Every Saturday, Harry goes down to the Bull Ring. He buys up all the flowers he can carry. Then I see him come out every Sunday morning, looking like a florist's shop. All dressed up in his black suit and bowler hat. He catches the no 5 down to Witton, and he has two pints at the *Safe Harbour*, one for him and one for George. Then he walks over to the cemetery and he puts the flowers on George's grave, and he has a little chat to him. Tells him how he misses him. Just like an old married couple."

She pauses again. My parents are silent.

"Every Sunday without fail."

After she goes, Dad says to Mom:

"I remember in the 1930s, I was just a lad, I walked past the Barton's Arms on my way home from school. There was a man outside there, very tall, and with a very posh accent. He was ranting on, the Jews are responsible for this and that and the other.

He said his name was Sir Oswald Mosley.

I was at school with some Jewish lads, and it didn't seem to me that they were responsible for what was wrong with our lives."

"No," says my mother, "it was the Government. Easy to blame it on others."

"Well, he offered us sixpence to join the Blackshirts. I took the sixpence and went off and bought an ice cream!"

They both laugh.

"Birmingham came right in the end," says my mother. "But I'm not saying that doesn't still happen. Or that it might not happen again. A government, a politician, that lays its own sins on an innocent group and whips up hatred against them."

25. In Arcadia, Ego

I am a happy child and I lead a happy life. We are in the fortunate position that everyone in the family is happy and healthy between 1957 – 1968. No-one gets divorced, no-one dies, nobody is really ever ill. It gives the decade a golden gleam, a patina of happiness which chimes well with the jaunty bounciness of the Sixties; the clothes, the music, the hairstyles, the general prosperity. No-one is even out of work; you can walk to any factory in Birmingham and get a job, day, evening, night shift.

However, sometimes even I am aware that everything is not so good for everyone, or that all is not well with the world, or well for everyone else. For example, there is a poor old man on the street whose legs are splayed out from the knees outwards, so that he looks half the size he is. He straddles along with an effort, legs bent out from the knee and the children run from him in pitiful horror.

"He had polio as a child," whispers my nan. "No treatment, you see."

The ladies at the hairdresser's keep their heads together one morning, whispering as they look at me and my sister.

"A monster .... A shapeless mass of flesh ... Just a head .... Tiny little arms and legs .... Better if it dies ...."

My mother will not tell us what they are talking about when we ask her on the way home. They were talking about a baby born around here, she says, and it is not well, but later we hear her whispering to my nan, and we hear a word we do not understand. Thalidomide?

My mother murmurs to my father, stories of depression, disease and death on the street – suicide. There is a man, Peter, who runs a little business in the Jewellery Quarter, one he has built up himself. Then he is forced out of business by larger businesses, more successful business men, and he is out of work – closes up his little workshop for the last time and hands back the keys.

"He could get a job at a factory," says my dad, "but it's hard when you've been your own boss. And they don't want to give a job on the line to a man who has been in charge."

His wife has a job as a dinner lady, and he has to sign on for the dole. That's the only time he goes out; no-one sees him. Then one day his wife arrives back from school to find the house full of gas and Peter slumped in his chair. He has turned on all the gas taps and killed himself.

My mother has a friend whose father suffered from depression *for no known reason*. Therefore he did not get any sympathy because *there is no known reason*, and the NHS is busy enough without dealing with mental health problems in the working classes.

"Then Betty came home from school one day, pushed open the door, and there he was, legs dangling," says my mother. "He stood on the table, attached a noose to the ceiling, jumped and hanged himself."

School is a very protected world. Perhaps because it is so small (only one hundred children in all), and it is easy for the teachers to maintain discipline. Mr Sims does not really believe in corporal punishment, which you still find at other schools, and the teachers only have to look at us for us to behave.

But some of the big children can be frightening, and they will do it behind the teachers' backs.

There is a big girl who torments me. Her name is Patricia, and she has a sly face and small eyes. She sits behind me in assembly, and she pulls the sash of my dress, or tugs at my short hair. I avoid her in the playground, but if she does see me, she puts her hand to her mouth and laughs and points.

I don't tell anyone about this because it is somehow shameful, and besides, even if she gets told off, she will still be at large to torment me in secret. I can only wait for her to leave.

Every day biscuits are sold in one of the classrooms at breaktime. Everyone wants to help with this – you can help yourself to the broken biscuits – but it is nearly always the big girls who do it, and Patricia is one of them.

Mrs Wardell co-ordinates the rota and one day she tells me with a kindly smile that because I have got a gold star for my reading, I can help on the biscuit sale rota instead of Patricia for a day.

I want to help – it looks such fun – but all the time I am in the classroom, selling biscuits and marshmallows, wrapped in tin foil, I am dreading seeing her.

Suddenly she appears in the queue. I duck down, but I can't stay there forever, and by the time she shuffles to the front, I am serving again. The glare she gives me is *deadly*.

"What's wrong?" says Mrs Wardell, concerned; but I shake my head.

It spoils my whole day; I go home at dinner time with a heavy heart and meditate on telling my mum that I am not feeling well, but she is too busy to notice; besides she never lets us miss school unless we are prostrate.

In afternoon playtime, I am walking around with Sandra, when a bunch of the big girls loom up in front of me. They all look a bit menacing, even pretty Lesley, who I admire from afar because she wears mini skirts.

"You need to go behind the toilets," says one of the girls. "Pat wants to see you."

They begin to shuffle me along. Sandra grabs my arm. I am *terrified*.

"Run!" shrieks Sandra, as terrified as me. "Run to the teacher!"

Mrs Burton is patrolling the playground, arms outstretched, a child clinging to each finger. I fight free, run to her, grab her hand. She glances down at me from under her headscarf and hornrims.

"What's wrong?" she asks, but I shake my head and cling to her hand for dear life.

From that day on, till she leaves, I avoid Patricia. I have learnt a sad lesson; *good people cannot always stop others from doing bad things.*

Sometimes, on a Saturday night, my father stands on the doorstep, looking over the road.

"I don't know whether to run down to the phone box and call the police," he says to my mother.

"Leave it," murmurs my mother uneasily. "I'll speak to her. You don't know what he might do to you."

My sister and I love Saturday night; we have a tea of egg and chips and baked beans on the baize table, and then we cuddle up on the sofa with our parents and watch *Voyage to the Bottom of the Sea*. Then my mother goes up the yard for the craic with my nan. My dad uncorks his Beer at Home means Davenport's and announces with a lordly air that we can stay up as long as we don't disturb him while he watches *Match of the Day*. Dad's taste in TV runs to Westerns and war films, so from an early age, my sister and I are viewing *Maverick* and *Bonanza*, *Rawhide* and *Sugarfoot*, *The Colditz Story* and *The Dam Busters* (to the point where we know the script better than they do). Mom's tastes run to cop shows and legal dramas.

In fact, although we have been told to be quiet, Dad is unable to refrain from a running commentary during *Match of the Day*, and we are his only audience, so we gamely join in. In this way, we discuss with him the offside rule, the respective merits of the Charlton brothers, Sir Alf's likely picks for the next England squad, and the dubious paternity of the referee.

Our ignorance is so appalling that Dad stirs himself to buy *Football for Girls* for me; it has a Sixties dolly bird on the front, gazing up adoringly at a handsome George Best type footballer. Susie gets *The Match of the Day Annual for Boys*.

At some point in the evening, my father emerges from his Davenport fuelled expert match analysis and announces that we had "better get up to bed before your mom gets home," and we scamper up the narrow winding stairs to our attic bedroom and fall asleep as only a contented child can.

One Saturday night we are awoken by noises outside and a blue flashing light. I tiptoe up to the window. There is a police car opposite and an ambulance. I can hear my parents moving around downstairs. My mum calls up to me:

"Get back to bed!"

It isn't for some years that I find out what has happened, when Mom tells me when I am much older.

"There was a girl lived opposite, you see, with her husband. He worked all week round, then he got his pay packet and he drank all weekend. Then he came home blind drunk and he beat her up.

That was why your dad wanted to go over and I wouldn't let him. The man was so rough and his mates were rough, so I worried they might harm your dad. So I went over and spoke to her. Said she needed to go, or speak to the police, or a nurse, or the doctor – anyone.

'Lil,' she said, 'I can't go anywhere. I've got nowhere to go. And if I speak to anyone, he'll deny it, and then he'll kill me.'

Then she got pregnant and had a baby – didn't stop him.

The baby cried a lot – we all heard it – not surprising in that house of hell.

One Saturday, the baby cried so much, she took it into bed with her. Then they both fell asleep.

He got home roaring drunk, fell onto the bed unconscious. Killed the baby."

"No", she says, when I question her further. He didn't get prosecuted – they said it was an accident.

"And do you know, they came round and had a collection for him, losing his baby! I slammed the door in their faces – he'll just take it down to the pub, I said, and come back and beat her up again."

I can't imagine how anyone would want to hurt a child. Nobody in my world would hurt a child – home and school are both such protected worlds.

Then for the first time ever, my parents, who let us read *everything*, are hiding the *Daily Mirror* from us. Mr Sims announces in Assembly that a policeman has come into school to give us a talk. The policeman stands up, tall and quite stout in his navy blue uniform and twisting his tall helmet in his hands. We are enjoying this; it is like the visit of the singing vicar. Maybe a talk on road safety and how to cross the road like in the Rufty Tufty Club?

But what he tells us makes us fall silent. He tells us that there are some bad people out there *and they are killing children*. This is in the north of England, but they don't know where the bad people come from. We must never speak to strangers, we must never accept sweets from strangers, we must never get into a stranger's car, and we must walk on the side of the pavement nearest to the houses, because if a car stops and someone talks to us, we must run to the nearest house and knock on the door. *Because if we go with a stranger, the stranger will kill us.*

We children are petrified by this talk and for weeks afterwards. At home, my parents don't let us watch the news or read the newspaper, but we are aware of a new terror in the air. It lasts for two years till the murderers are caught, and at last we see the faces of Brady and Hindley, the Moors Murderers, staring out from the front page of the *Daily Mirror*. And it is perhaps truthful to say that every child of the Sixties never felt that life was the same again. *Some people kill children.*

"They should bring back the death penalty," grunts my father.

"For child murders, but not for everyone," counters my mother. "What about Ruth Ellis?"

"She killed a man, didn't she?"

"No," says my mother, "she executed him."

If it wasn't enough for my parents to deal with, there are a series of child murders in Birmingham, known as the Cannock Chase murders. This is near to home, as one of the victims is from Aston!

The friendly policeman comes to visit us again, but my mother has already sprung into action. Whereas they don't discuss the Moors Murders in front of us, we hear all about the Cannock Chase Murders, and besides, they are all over the *Birmingham Mail*. We see all the headlines on the vendors' boards as we come out of school, and they shout:

"Ge – et your Evening Mail! Cannock Chase murders latest!"

My mother rams the message home:

"If you speak to a stranger, you might get killed. If a stranger offers you sweets, you might get killed. If you get into a stranger's car, you will be killed."

Playing on the street is now forbidden; like every other child, we disappear into the house, or we play up the back yard. We don't go anywhere alone. My mother organises a phalanx of family to march us to and from school six times every day.

It strikes close to home as well. Both my father and my Uncle Bill now drive Cambridge A60s, a huge tank of a car. There is a rumour that the murderer might drive a grey Austin and the police interview every single driver of a grey Austin. For the first time ever, a policeman calls at our house on a Saturday morning and my sister and I are frightened. My mother sends us upstairs while he questions my father.

"It was easy for your Dad," she says later. "He's got witnesses, he's at work. But poor Uncle Bill, he was a lorry driver and he was really worried, because half the time, no-one knew where he was at all."

For years, I can never think of Cannock Chase as a lovely place for a day out. I just think of it as a place where children were murdered and buried. And my mother can never forget the fate of Margaret Reynolds, the little girl from Aston.

"It could have been anyone," she sighs. "I can even remember the day I heard of it and what you two were wearing. It could have been you."

My mother and my nan like to go to the cemetery on the No 5 bus and put flowers on Grandad's grave. They don't take us – we don't see it for years, until a terrible day in 1970 – because my nan says it is "not suitable for children".

"Enough sadness in the world already," she says.

It's not that they seem sad, because they come back talking about Grandad, telling little anecdotes about him.

My father is envious; he has very few memories of his parents that are happy. He remembers his mother, worn out by childbirth, screaming in agony as she dies of stomach cancer, the family unable to afford any pain relief. He remembers his father descending into drink, the children running wild, begging for food, dressed in ragged clothes and the hated *Daily Mail* boots, selling lumps of coal dropped from the coal lorry.

"All the same, I would like to find their graves," he reflects.

One Saturday he accompanies my mother to the cemetery and calls at the little lodge by the Moor Lane entrance. He can give them his parents' names and the year of their deaths, but not much more.

"It's a pauper's grave," whispers the lodge attendant, clearly embarrassed.

It takes my father some time to find the small grave, in that part of the cemetery reserved for those who cannot afford a burial. The co-op, who bury everyone in Birmingham provide a special package for the common grave. It is overgrown, no marker or headstone, surrounded by a little stone border.

My father can do anything with his hands. He asks permission at the lodge, and then he comes down every Saturday or Sunday, on his day off. He clears up the neglected grave; he plants a little flower bed with bulbs to bloom every spring, he installs – with some effort – a heavy stone pot for flowers, and he plants a beautiful rose bush, which flowers every year till the year he dies.

One sunny Sunday morning, we are having a full breakfast on the old green table – beans, bacon, sausage, egg and fried bread which is my favourite, especially if I put brown sauce on. My sister and I have a cup of tea, which apart from squash is really all we drink. Mom buys us each a can of White's lemonade to go with Sunday dinner, which we love, but on the whole she does not approve of fizzy drinks.

Dad has made himself a rather exotic coffee, from a little bottle called Camp's. It has a picture on the front of a turbanned Indian serving coffee to a British officer. A relict of the British empire which no longer exists, says Dad, which is a good thing because it did nothing for the working classes. But the coffee smells lovely, much better than it tastes – we have a sip, and it is so bitter.

He is telling my mum about his work on the grave.

"It's so good I think I'll be buried there!" he finishes.

My mother says tartly that she intends to be buried in her father's grave, and she thought he would go there too.

"Well, that's alright. You go with your parents, I'll go with mine and then I'll come over and see you every Sunday!"

Then they both laugh. Death seems very far away on that bright Spring morning. *Et in Arcadia ego.*

26. Heroes and Heroines

My mother likes to see the Royal Family. She can remember coming out of work on the day of the Royal Wedding in 1947, and buying the *Evening Mail* with the photos in. She goes to the cinema to see the film of the Coronation.

Her heroine is Barbara Castle. "I love her hair and clothes," she sighs and quickly adds that she also approves of Barbara's policies. They call her The Red Queen and my mother reads admiringly of her in the *Daily Mirror*.

Her heroes are rather unlikely ones: Muhammad Ali, Alex Higgins, George Best and John Lennon. There's something about their maverick personalities that thrills her conventional soul, and of course they are outstanding examples of male beauty.

My father's heroes are Harold Wilson and Sir Alf Ramsey; he buys the *Daily Mirror* because it is Labour, and also because it has pictures of his heroes. He has a picture of Harold on one wall and Sir Alf and the Boys of '66 on another, and on Saturday nights he raises his Beer at Home means Davenport to them.

Of course, we think our mothers and fathers are heroes and heroines, but at least once in their life, they are truly heroic.

I have been afflicted with catarrh since birth, as my sister has bronchitis. Maybe it's the smog of Birmingham, the factories pouring out smoke which mingles with the fog, so that in the Autumn we have to go to school with a torch with scarves wrapped over our mouths and noses to keep out the swirling yellow smoke, or maybe it's just the fact that everyone smokes.

In any case, my earaches get worse to the point where I bang my head against the wall to keep out the pain, and then they notice. I haven't said anything about it before. It is somehow shameful to be *ill*. Then I develop tonsillitis, months and months of it in a particularly bitter winter with snow on the ground. I am too prostrate to go to school and my mother lets me lie on the sofa while she spoons liquids down my throat.

"I don't want anything, 'cos it hurts," I sob, and I become thinner than ever.

"Well, that's it," says my mother and she calls in at the surgery to tell Dr Carolan that I must have my tonsils out. Dr Carolan signs the forms as he puffs on his Woodbine and coughs. No-one defies my mother when she is rampant, so the obliging Dr Carolan – Eddie – who goes to the greyhounds every Saturday night with my Uncle John, arranges it, so there you go.

The NHS is actually going through a stage of thinking it is good to rip out children's tonsils, so they are quite amenable and the typewritten letter arrives, ordering me to arrive at the Children's Hospital on Tuesday afternoon; operation Wednesday, discharge on Thursday.

This letter causes a bit of a quandary.

"We can take her on the bus," says Nan, shaking her head, "and John can pick Susie up from school. But she can't come home on the bus in bitter weather and a sore throat."

After some discussion my father, for the first time ever, arranges a half day off work so he can fetch me in the car, and of course, he'll lose half a day's pay.

"Well, I'll do the Saturday morning or the Friday afternoon at Lucas's to make it up," says my mother.

On the appointed morning, after Susannah is walked to school, my mother and nan bundle me up against the cold in leggings, coat, hat, gloves and scarf, and clutching a little bag with my pyjamas and teddy and a book in, we catch the no 5 into Birmingham. Then in compliment to my illness, we catch a second bus along Broad St to the Children's Hospital instead of walking. Actually, I would like to walk and look at the shops; I don't get into Birmingham too often.

At the hospital I am given a bed, and change into my pyjamas and a hospital dressing gown and slippers – in the afternoon!

"Now say goodbye to your mummy and nanny," directs a rather fierce looking nurse in a starched uniform.

Their faces are so stricken as they kiss me goodbye that I can hardly stop myself from bursting into tears. We have *never* been separated. But then, as my nan always says, crying does you no good and so I manage a wobbly wave as they walk off, looking back. Because we don't have a phone this is the last they will see of me till Thursday.

Tea is a rather subdued affair, presided over by the nurses. All the children are rather frightened. I can't eat the tea, as it is pasteurised milk and marmalade sandwiches which I don't have at home, and the nurses say I am a naughty little girl.

The next day (and I don't sleep well in the high ceilinged, draughty ward full of sobbing children), I am wheeled down *first* by some very pleasant ward orderlies, who tell me jokes.

The surgeon seems terrifying, all dressed in white, but he is nice as he tells me it's just a *small* needle going into my hand and I'll be asleep before he finishes counting one ... two ... three ....

Then I wake up and I am screaming, "Mom! Mom!" My throat is *raw*, and the nurses are moving me back into my bed.

"Stop it, you're frightening the other children!" scolds the cross nurse and I stop instantly. I am programed to obey authority.

Eating is impossible, and as I have two weeks off school to convalesce, I am to go home that very afternoon, and Dad is coming to fetch me in the car. I am so small and thin that he can carry me.

"She'll soon put on weight now," say the nurses brightly.

The reception committee is made up of my mum and my nan, peering out the door as he carries me up the step and lays me on the sofa in our small room. I am swathed in blankets and shawls. I am, after all, *ill*.

Apart from having a throat which feels like a broken glass, and thinking that I am probably never going to eat or drink again, I quite enjoy being fussed over as my mum and nan are not "ones for making a fuss" usually.

Suddenly there is a huge commotion outside, shouting and screaming; instantly all three rush out and leave me alone. I'm too weak to get up and look out the window, and it is freezing outside.

After what seems like forever, my parents come back – Nan has gone to get Susie from school – and they seem to be in a state of shock. Dad falls into the armchair – his face is all covered in something black – and Mom goes off to boil the kettle so he can wash and have a cup of tea. Dad is shaking his head, over and over.

It is some time before we find out what has happened, and by that time Dad has his picture in the *Evening Mail!*

Deaths by fire and by gas in the street are legendary. People have been gassed to death by faulty gas systems, electrocuted by faulty electric fittings, and whole families have been wiped out by fires. The houses are tall and thin, and the children often sleep on the top floor, and as fire rages through the house, the kids are wiped out before the fire engine arrives. Someone will have to run to the nearest public phone box to call 999, and as like as not, it has been vandalised. My mother can remember an entire family of six children and their rescuer killed in such a way in the 1930s, and they are all buried in a mass grave in Witton.

A little old lady a few houses up fell asleep on the sofa while smoking, and the cigarette soon sets the cheap sofa alight. Within minutes, the house is ablaze and smoke is pouring out the windows. Someone runs off to find the phone box, but that's when my dad and the postie kick the door down, rush in and grab her – she's unconscious from the smoke – and pull her out.

"With difficulty," reflects my dad, "as her skin was turning black and coming off. And useless, since she died in hospital."

In any case, he and the postie get their photos in the paper, and the kids at school say to us, "Your dad's a hero!"

The police come round to ask if Dad wants to be nominated for a medal, but he shakes his head. What's the use? The family has stacks of war medals from my grandfathers and as my mother says, they didn't put bread into our mouths.

No, of much more concern to the family is that Dad has lost a half day's pay fetching me from the hospital, and so before the end of the month, my mother, who is now working evenings, volunteers to do a Friday morning at Lucas's. There is always stacks of overtime and it fits in between our school hours.

On the appointed day, she drops us off at school and sets off to Great Hampton Street, where she is now working. It is further to walk, but she likes it better than Great King Street. It is a much older building, set on a corner. My mother works on B Line on the first floor.

My mother takes in her lunch and tea in a large thermos flask. The bottom of it unscrews, and you can put in a tiny bottle of milk, and sugar in a screw of paper. She takes in the *Daily Mirror* to read. She doesn't know anyone on the day shift, so she remains at her machine at lunch break, smoking, reading, gazing out of the window.

There is a bank opposite, on the corner of the street. As my mother gazes, a van draws up outside it. A gang of men erupt from it – she gets a good view as they stop to pull on masks – and surely they are carrying arms? What is this?

My mother's eyes widen. She hesitates, then she rises from her machine to call Steve, the foreman, who comes running – he dashes off to Mr Laker's office to use the phone. This is wonderful! This is just like *Z Cars* on the telly! But by the time the police arrive, The Gang, as they are christened in the local media, have driven off with the contents of the bank's vaults.

My mother is the only witness, and the only person to have seen their faces. She is interviewed at some length by the police when they arrive, which she rather enjoys; she loves cop shows on the telly.

In fact, The Gang are caught red handed within days, as to be honest they are pretty amateur.

There is to be a big show trial at Birmingham's Victoria Crown Courts and my mother is the star witness! The kids at school are really impressed. "Your mum's in the paper!"

My grandmother is a bit ambivalent about all this. She thinks a lady's name appears only three times in the paper: hatches, matches and dispatches. Besides, she thinks my mother is *loving* the attention: she is looking forward to going to court and seeing the judge and all the barristers in the courtroom because she loves *Perry Mason* on the telly.

"I'd better go with her," sighs my grandmother reluctantly.

For their great court date, my nan and mum draw out their post office savings and buy new outfits: hats, gloves, bags, shoes, and neat coats and skirts.

"They'll do for the next family wedding," says my mother, to justify this extravagance; nobody would ever dream of turning up at a family wedding in an outfit that wasn't completely new. People would think you were *poor*.

On the day, the entire street turns up to see them leave no 37 for their date with destiny; their regal exit is rather marred by the fact that they don't leap into a limousine but walk up to Summer Lane in their finery to catch the no 7 bus.

In spite of herself, my nan does enjoy the spectacle of Birmingham Crown Court; of course, she has been there many a time as a cleaner, as Great Uncle Jack is caretaker there and he slips in with Aunty Lil to watch the proceedings.

The whole thing is over in a day. The Gang were caught red handed, loot still in the van, but my mother was the only one to see their faces and she is called to identify them as they stand in the dock.

She destroys the prosecution – she has 20/20 vision thank you very much, and she tells her story, contemptuously, swatting off the prosecution like a buzzing fly.

"And at the end," says my grandmother, "the Gang stood in the dock and shook their fists and they vowed to get her when they came out if it took the rest of their lives!"

Of course, with robbery under arms, the sentence is a hefty one and they are going to be doddering when they do get out – she could probably slay them with a glance – but Uncle John takes delight for years in coming in and saying "The Gang are out and they're waiting down on the street corner for you!"

Afterwards my mother and grandmother walk out in the sunshine onto the front steps of the court. A phalanx of photographers and journalists are waiting for them and the cameras begin to pop.

My mother raises one gloved hand in acknowledgement of the crowd, twisting it at the wrist as she has seen the Queen do. She turns her haughty head from side to side; she pirouettes slowly to show her clothes; she poses for the cameras.

Behind my mother, my nan hides her face behind her bag.

But my mother is radiant. This is her hour. This is her fifteen minutes of fame.

27. The Last Year

It seems that everything begins to change very suddenly. The sunny world of the street and William Cowper Junior and Infant School, has been my world for ten years. Utopia on one of Birmingham's poorest council estates.

But now everything is changing. The Sixties are nearly over. As people move out of the street, the houses are boarded up and the council come round and take photographs of them. The street looks like a mouth where half the teeth are rotten. It's because all of the terraced back to backs are going to be demolished. The council is building big new estates.

My father tells me we will be moving to a house with three bedrooms, front and back gardens, a bathroom and inside toilet, and hot running water and central heating!

We are amongst the last to go because I am sitting the eleven plus in February 1968. Or so my mother says. Really we are the last to go because she is holding out for a council house in the area where we live; she won't go anywhere else, and she won't be separated from my nan.

A lady from the council comes round to the house and tells them a whole new estate is being built close by called the Newtown Estate, between Summer Lane and Newtown Row. They will also be building high rise blocks of flats there for older people and my nan can have one of those. She will have her very own bedroom, a bathroom and a balcony to sit and enjoy the sun.

We are due to go in the summer of 1968. The rent will be much higher than the fifteen shillings a week we pay now. But my father says that the foreman at work is due to retire next year, and he will be made foreman and get a higher wage.

He will recommend Johnnie Murray to be chargehand. He says he will do the Open University in Management at Brooklyn Technical College. He is also planning to do a course in Public Speaking at the Brasshouse Centre, as he will be representing the firm.

"People laugh at Brummie accents, and they think we're thick," he explains.

This puzzles me as both my parents, who left school at the age of fourteen, are very clever and can read and write fluently, and do arithmetic in their head. They have done loads of Trade Union courses as shop stewards. Why should people judge them on their accents?

My father has something else on his mind. He thinks Harold Wilson's government is limping towards inevitable defeat in the 1970 election. He is going to leave the Labour Party and focus on his career.

On 27th August 1967: the death of Brian Epstein is announced on the radio.

"That's the end of the Beatles," says my father. "They won't go on without him."

They do limp on for another couple of years, but they never seem the same; more troubled now, more rebellious, no longer the smartly dressed Fab Four with their gleaming hair and gleaming boots. They too seem to look forward to a less happy time. My mother no longer buys their singles. All the groups of the Sixties are breaking up. There are other sounds on the radio.

There's another big change coming. My father has written to Mrs Bricknell at the farm about her holidays. She writes back to say this will be her last year at the farm, but we are very welcome. The lease has expired and the owner wants them to move out, so he can turn it into an hotel.

My parents are sorry about this, but they think that next year, they may go to a holiday camp, where we will stay in a chalet and there will be things for us to do, and they can go to the club every night and see a cabaret.

Everything is different at school as well. I have been in Top Class for two years with Mr Tapper. He is a short, brisk Welshman with gleaming brown eyes; he always wears a tweed jacket and cord trousers. He doesn't read to us like Mrs Burton did, but he does give us inspiring little pep talks. One day he says to us that he can't understand why the British are so prejudiced against people with darker skins when they themselves lie on beaches burning themselves brown all day.

This is food for thought.

In my second year in Top Class, everything is different. I don't do art, swimming, scripture, needlework, recorders or dance anymore. Instead, after Assembly, some of us are taken off to a separate classroom. Here we sit all day and work our way through old eleven plus papers with Mr Sims. At this point I begin to realise that everyone is concerned about how really, really bad

I am at maths. I am appalling. I sit gazing at the maths papers with tears streaming down my face.

Nobody can understand it; my parents can do sums in their head and my sister is very quick. It begins to dawn on everyone *that I might fail the eleven plus.*

Emergency measures are put into place. My parents used to go to a youth club run by the Quakers when they were young and sometimes the former Youth Leader, Bob Slack, calls in at the house.

"Maybe I can get her into the Quaker School," he offers.

My mother also says to my dad:

"Your dad was a Catholic convert ... maybe you can tell the Catholic school and get her into that."

Nobody in my family is devout. It's just that the faith schools are thought to have better care.

Mr Sims comes up with another solution; the eleven plus contingent will sit the exam for Art School, which is another option. Our art lessons, abruptly stopped, now start again. One Saturday morning, Mr Sims takes us on the bus to Marsh Hill Grammar, where we sit in a big classroom, painting two pictures. One has to be called *The Invaders,* and I design what I think is a very sophisticated picture of giant green caterpillars chomping the flowers. The other has to be called *The Dancers,* and so I just paint a picture of a beautiful ballerina in pink, because I love all my ballet books.

Mr Tapper leaves us at Christmas. He is going down to be head of a school in Cornwall. He tells us that Cornwall is just like Wales; once a separate country, its own kings and queens, its own language.

We have a collection with whatever pennies we can spare, and give the money to Mrs Wardell; she buys him a fountain pen, which Philip presents to him in class with a polite speech, blushing up to the hair roots as he does it, but manfully struggling through.

Mr Tapper is replaced by Mr Hindle, a gentle Evangelical Christian, who tells us Bible stories from little magazines called Keynotes. He can also speak French and he teaches us a few phrases.

Mrs Burton thinks the eleven plus class are working very hard, and she offers to take us on an expedition. For two shillings and sixpence each, we are going to take two buses to the Arts Centre in Cannon Hill Park to see a play called *The Servant of Two Masters.*

Although I go to the cinema and we have a travelling play company come into school every year, this is the first time I have ever been to the theatre and I love it; the stage, the curtains, the costumes and the play itself, which revolves around the adventures of a rascally servant. Mrs Burton tells us that Tommy Steele played the part in London and we are really impressed because he is a Big Star.

By a horrible coincidence, the eleven plus falls on my eleventh birthday, which is a Wednesday. I can't believe this. It will spoil my day and I know I am getting what I really want: a gold (or rather rolled gold) locket. My dad has been up to the Jewellery Quarter to get it. It's because all the heroines in my comics wear lockets which are clues to their real identities; a princess, a duke's daughter, captured at birth and taken away to live with the gypsies.

On the appointed day, I get up feeling sick. It has snowed this winter, and we have been out in our coats and boots and hats and scarves, throwing snowballs and making snowmen in the yard. But today it is just icy cold. In bed, you lie quite still with all the blankets and sheets and the candlewick counterpane heaped on you; you never make a gap for a draught. The windows, if not iced up, are running with water every morning and my dad has to go round with towels, sopping it all up. You would never get out of bed without putting your dressing gown and slippers on.

"Better open your cards and presents when you get home," says my mother encouragingly. "Then you can spend more time on it."

She forces a bowl of porridge down me because she thinks it is sustaining. I quite like it with extra milk and sugar. Anyway, it means you don't feel the cold so much as we roll along to school, in about ten layers of clothing. My sister and I, because we are considered to be frail, also have to wear button up leggings and a horrible scratchy woolly vest called a Liberty bodice.

Top Class don't have Assembly on this morning; we go straight to a classroom where we are sat down. The inkwells are full, a wooden pen with a nib attached is placed on each desk, but mainly now we write with blue biros.

We have two papers to write, Maths and English. English is first, which cheers me up; there are lots of general questions, like giving the plurals or opposites of words and putting sentences in the right order. Then you have to choose an essay to write; I pick one called *Locked in the Zoo at Night*, which offers all sorts of scope for exciting adventures with me as the heroine. We call this Composition in school and I love writing.

The maths isn't actually as bad as I had dreaded because I have done so much practice.

After the eleven plus, life returns to normal. I forget all about it until the day when Mrs Wardell comes into the classroom and asks for five of the children to go to Mr Sims's office.

We stand ranged around his desk; three boys, two girls. Half the class. The Chosen.

"Well children, your parents will be getting a letter in the post, but I am very pleased to tell you that you have passed the eleven plus and you will be offered a place at Grammar School. Well done, a credit to the school!"

It is a Friday and I can hardly wait to get home and tell my mum. But I wait till Dad gets home and then I tell both of them.

My dad is ecstatic. He himself was not able to go to Grammar School in 1939 because he could not afford the uniform. But they have plenty saved up in the Post Office for me.

My dad breaks out a rare cigar, bought from the off licence. "I'm going to get her into King Edward's, the best Grammar School in Birmingham!"

He knows – he has a mate who works for the Council – that comprehensive education is coming in, but that the King Edward's Schools are going to refuse to change. As my family had no education at all till the 1870s, and then was fobbed of with inner city schools and an early school leaving age – to make them improved factory fodder who can read and write – my father does not see why his girls cannot have the best.

I am to be a real schoolgirl, just like in my comics, with a school uniform and satchel, and I will learn French and Latin.

He has news of his own.

"The foreman announced today he's going. Management had me in and told me I'm to be next foreman, so I get a pay rise, and they're paying for me to go to Brooklyn Tech Night School in September and do Management! I asked for Johnnie Murray to be made chargehand."

He is leaving the Labour Party and the Trade Union he says. He now has other things to do.

My mother has news too. She is waving a letter from Birmingham City Council.

"Floss and Bert had one too, they're going to a maisonette in Five Ways. We've got a council house in Newtown and Mom's got a flat on the estate!"

More celebrations. Floss and Bert come round and my nan comes down the entry. My dad says he will fetch fish and chips for us all, and break open a couple of Davenports, while my nan passes round cigarettes and my mother puts the kettle on.

While this happening, I slip quietly to the door and look out at the sunny street no different than ten years ago, but now with so many houses empty. Soon we will all be gone, and the street will disappear under a new council estate. 1970 will bring an election and a new Government. I have heard a record on the radio today, a curious song called *Major Tom,* by someone called David Bowie; different from any music I have ever heard before. Some of the local cinemas are closing too, as people stay home and watch the telly more. We have a new channel called ITV and also BBC Two. William Cowper School itself is to go and be replaced by a brand new building. The Seventies are upon us.

And as in 1961 I stood at this very door, gazing out into the sunlit street and wondering what school would be like and what the Sixties would bring, I now gaze out and wonder what the new house will be like, the new school, what the Seventies will bring, and will I ever again be as happy as I was as a child in Guildford Street?

28. The Last Days

Things seem to move very quickly then. A letter arrives from Birmingham City Council announcing that I have won a Grammar School place. There is a form to fill in and my dad has to put five grammar schools down. He puts King Edward's Handsworth first. It is a girls' Grammar School.

A letter arrives from them, asking me to come for an interview. It is on thick cream paper and the envelope has the school coat of arms embossed on it. It is signed by Miss P. Reid, MA, Headmistress.

I have an afternoon off school for the interview and my mother dresses us in our very best. We catch the no 5 into Birmingham from Summer Lane, and then a no 74 bus to Handsworth.

"You'll be coming this way every day," says my mother. Four buses a day! How will they afford the bus fare?

King Edward's is situated in a small street off the Soho Rd. It is a beautiful, red brick building, with two flights of stairs leading to the entrance. My mother gives my name to the Receptionist, and we are asked to sit outside Miss Reid's office. We have to cross it to reach her desk, where I perch on a chair, my feet not touching the ground.

Miss Reid, who is Scottish, is tall and thin, has a very posh voice and wears a black gown over her dress. I am so overwhelmed by the entire experience that I can hardly say a word, but my mother praises all the wonderful things I can do.

"I think you'll find that *all* our girls are very clever," says Miss Reid loftily.

She tells us that she was a teacher at Benenden and that she taught Princess Anne. The council estate girl is going to be taught by someone who taught royalty.

Despite this, we do get a letter to say I have been accepted at the school, so I don't have any more interviews. I do have to go to a Parents' Evening in the huge Great Hall where we hear all about the school as a hundred and twenty new girls eye each other up warily. A hundred and twenty in one year! There are only fifty in the whole of William Cowper!

My parents get a full uniform list which includes things like navy blue leotards and swimming costumes, to be bought direct from the school. My mother takes me off to Grey's Department Store for the rest of the items; a King Edward's tie, two pinafores, shirts, navy blue socks, a blue mac, and a beret. My dad goes off to the Midland Educational Stores to get me a satchel and stationery. He has a manager at work whose daughter was at King Edward's and he generously donates much of her sports kit, including hockey boots and a hockey stick. My parents' Post Office savings account is just about wiped out. As they are both working, we don't qualify for a grant towards my uniform, and they are going to have to pay for my school meals as well.

In the meantime my parents are making arrangements to move. We are going in July, just after school finishes, so I will have a summer in the new house before I start school.

The last term at school is so sad. We don't do *Singing Together* any more; we just clear out the classrooms, throwing out all our old work books, although the best ones are kept as examples. I help Mrs Francis clear out the art room, throwing out all our old paintings. I take in my newly acquired autograph book and get everyone's autographs. We swap addresses, promising to write to each other (no-one has a phone). I help Mrs Burton tidy up the school library.

"You can come back and see us one day," she says.

She wants to keep all the stories I have written in my Composition book "as a souvenir and to read to the other children."

The travelling play company come in and do a play called *Just Imagine!* but I don't enjoy it as much as usual. It seems somehow suddenly childish.

"You'll be doing Shakespeare soon, and going on trips to the big theatre in Birmingham!" says Mrs Burton.

We have a final Sports Day, where I come last in the sack race. But suddenly sack races, egg and spoon, and obstacle races also seem childish. I am going to be playing hockey, netball and lacrosse.

On the last day when we break up at lunchtime, most of Top Class are in tears in Assembly. In class as we tidy up, Mr Hindle says a prayer for us. And then the noon bell rings and school is out for ever. Sandra is weeping.

We have our very last holiday at the farm; next year we are off to Cornwall and a holiday camp.

When we get back, Floss and Bert are gone and the house is boarded up.

My parents have hired a van to move our few sticks of furniture. Everything has to go to New John St West, as with the increase in rent, and my school uniform, there is no money for anything new. So the movers have to take the windows out to get the beds and wardrobes out.

My mother has walked round to the new house with my sister to open up with the new keys. So now the house is empty and there's just me and my dad putting a few things in the car.

"Come on, bab" he says.

My sister and I have already said goodbye to the yard. My nan will be following us in a few days.

He locks the door and posts the keys through the letter box. He fixes up a notice saying *Gone Away*, and Sellotapes the postbox shut. He has already spoken to the postman – his companion in the burning house adventure – about re-directing the post.

I get into the car beside him and we drive off. I turn and look over my shoulder at the street, bathed in the afternoon sunshine; a five minute drive, but a whole world away.

Requiem –
the well-loved dead

They're both gone now.

They exist only in a smiling photograph on my mantelpiece, in our memories, in a few boxes of family photographs and memorabilia in my loft.

I myself am sixty and it's not just my parents and my nan who are gone, but so many uncles and aunts, and indeed the whole way of life of the Birmingham back to backs.

My grandmother moved shortly after us into a neat flat in a high rise on the Newtown estate. She had two years to enjoy her balcony, her bedroom, her fitted kitchen, her very own bathroom and the hot running water and under-floor central heating, and she had two years to enjoy "Mr Lloyd George's old age pension".

Then on a terrible day in 1970, she is drying cutlery in our kitchen after Sunday lunch. Suddenly, she keels backwards, falling straight to the floor; dead of a clot to the brain that might have been floating around her body since her heart operation in the nineteen fifties. She is dead long before she gets to hospital; indeed she is dead before she hits the floor. The National Health Service cannot save her any more than it did her Mr Bevan, dead at sixty-two of stomach cancer.

My mother has a nervous breakdown which lasts on and off for several years; she lies in a darkened room sobbing while we tiptoe around and take care of ourselves. My father does not know how to cope with her. It is the end of our sunny childhood.

I begin to turn to the world of my grammar school. My teachers are encouraging; they say I am a clever girl and I should stay on into the Sixth Form and then University! I am on my way, the first person in my family to go to University, the first professional, the first generation not to become factory fodder.

Of course, in the end, my mother recovers, although by then we have grown away from her, we have our own lives to get on with. Happy times do lie ahead of them; they buy their council house, they buy a colour TV, they get a better car, they begin to go on holiday abroad. They watch their children go into the professions; they watch their grandchildren grow up. They both retire after fifty years in a factory with scarcely a day missed. But I often think that their happiest days were in the Sixties, in a terraced council house, when life was so simple.

I don't think that they had any regrets. They enjoyed their life and got on with it. I do ask them, just once:

"If you could have done anything at all that you wanted, what would you have chosen?"

Dad says:

"I love history. I think I would have read History at University and become a History teacher."

It is true that when we went to the public library, he borrowed lots of history books and so educated himself. Indeed, in his retirement he reads even more and takes evening classes in Spanish, English Language, Family History and use of computers. The boy who passed the eleven plus and left school at fourteen.

My mother says:

"I love the law... if I hadn't even been able to be a lawyer, I would have gone to commercial college and become a clerk to a lawyer."

Just what her father wanted for her in fact, except that he died in the war and she had to leave school, where she was always in the top stream, and go to work in a factory.

There are still days when I wake up and for a minute think that I must phone and see how they are; that there is something on TV that they would like to see, that there is a book coming out that Dad would like to read. Then I remember. All I can give them now is six feet of earth, a marble tomb and the occasional bunch of flowers. I stand in front of it, my arms stretched out to them across the void, but there is no answer and it is oh so sad! The rest is silence.

I set off and drive around the places I used to know.

Life changes in the Seventies. The old terraced houses, the narrow streets they stood in, are razed to the ground and big new council estates appear. The old Victorian primary schools are replaced by flat topped single-storey buildings. The washing baths close down; some of the swimming baths go too. Slowly, the old cinemas are replaced by multiscreen chains devoid of any character or architectural interest. The city planners hate Victoriana and they are going to get rid of it. The great Reference Library is flattened. The factories stand derelict and abandoned with broken windows as manufacturing ceases; buildings through which thousands of lives passed. Tucker Fasteners is closed and empty, the workforce pensioned off, manufacturing moved abroad. I pass by it when it first closes, wondering if there is anything left of my dad in it; I see photographs on the internet of darkened tool rooms, coats still hanging on racks, tea mugs left on shelves. The archive, with the history of the firm, in disarray. The traces of ourselves that we leave behind.

But one day it is gone completely.

Johnnie Murray says:

"They were supposed to save the clock tower. But on the first day of demolition, it was the first thing that went."

Lucas's Great King Street, gone, a derelict site in the middle of an abandoned park where nobody plays. Lucas's Great Hampton Street, where I can look up and see the window where my mother sat when she witnessed the bank robbery. The former factory is now a chic urban apartment block.

Cox's Optician's, the building still there, now boarded up. Dr Carolan's terraced surgery replaced by a Seventies Health Centre.

Birchfield Library, gone. They flattened it and said they would build a new one and they didn't. Aston Library, Aston Cross Library, closed; all those magical places full of wonderful books that shaped the imagination of an inner city child.

I would drive down the Lozells Rd, but I know all the shops that we went to are long gone and that the Villa Cross picture house with its huge stained glass rose window was burnt down.

Down from Six Ways, to Newtown Row; the Orient Cinema long gone.

Down Newtown Row; the Barton's Arms still standing, now a gastropub, but the clock hands have not moved for years. All the shops I knew on the Newtown Row, long gone, replaced with a Seventies precinct. The Aston Hippodrome, a Victorian palace where my parents saw Laurel and Hardy, demolished.

Guildford Street, now Guildford Drive, a Seventies council estate. I wonder why the hill to the Lozells Rd, which always seemed so big, is actually so small; maybe it's just that we were small and the world was big. I have seen so few pictures of Guildford Street; all our photographs were taken in the back yard. So I go to the Central Library and ask in Local Studies if they have any photographs of Guildford Street in the Sixties, and they say yes, they have something called the urban regeneration project or something like that – I can't quite catch it – the council went round and took pictures of the houses and streets to be demolished. And then they produce a photograph of our house.

The date is on it – June 1968 – it must have been taken right after we went. It is all boarded up and you can see where the removal men took out the windows to get the beds and furniture out. You can also see the unknown bush flowering in the front garden.

All quite gone, although as I drive up Geach Street to Summer Lane, I notice the Geach Street sign on the corner, opposite the church where we went briefly and unsuccessfully to Sunday School. It's fixed to the ground, the same one that was there when we walked up that way to school, so maybe that's why they haven't moved it and the corner is missing, but it's one of the very few things left.

Summer Lane, full of empty and boarded up businesses. Many of the pubs are gone, or look down at heel; there are no shops left, apart from White's Ironmongery, its windows still full of the hardware that my dad loved to buy. But the shop has been locked up for a long time.

The Birmingham Settlement, where we went to Brownies and my mother to jumble sales, moved to another address.

Saddest of all, the site where William Cowper School stood. It was demolished in 1972; it was quite a sight when the steeple was toppled and I go down with Dad to see it. The school is already half gone, standing open; I can see the hall and the classrooms and the balconies and the huge overarching roof.

At the actual moment when the wrecking ball swings and the steeple goes over, I can't bear to watch and I turn away.

On the way home, I say:

"Why do they do it, Dad? Why do they demolish all the buildings we care about?"

My father says:

"Nobody cares about working class heritage."

Houses, shops, schools, factories, markets, cinemas, pubs, parks, swimming baths ... all gone. Heritage, only for the affluent. The National Trust crowd.

My father died in 2008. He had battled prostate cancer for a long time and successfully. Then he develops clots on his lungs and they stop the treatment.

Possibly a legacy of so many years spent in smoky rooms says the doctor, or maybe the buildings he worked in were full of asbestos.

He suffers dreadfully, to the point where my aunt prays for him to die and be released from his agony. I have him moved to a hospice, where his life dwindles to one narrow room. But they give him morphine, lots of it, so at least he is no longer screaming aloud in agony as his mother did when she died. The NHS can at least do that much for him.

I visit him the night before he dies. He has been lying comatose for weeks, eyes closed, nothing there. But as far as I know, not in pain. Before I go, I lean over, kiss him, smooth his hair, wish him a good night. "See you in the morning," I say.

He opens his eyes, wide and blue and gives me, for just a few seconds, a radiant smile. Then his eyes close and he is gone again.

He dies in the night and my sister and I weep at his bedside the morning after. He looks like a young man again, all the lines of pain smoothed out, but the alarm clock will never sound for him again, as it did for fifty years, to summon him to work; or after that, in his retirement, to help his wife and daughters, to his hobbies and his interests, to his holidays and his days out with his grandchildren.

I dream about him the night before his funeral, which is odd because I never dream. My sister and I are walking down Guildford Street hand in hand with him; we are grown women, as we are now, but he is a young man again, in his smart suit.

"Look after your mother," he says, and then, "I'll be with you tomorrow but you won't be able to see me."

Then he lets go of our hands and walks off without looking back.

My mother cannot cope after the death of my father. I arrange several counsellors for her, from the hospice or from Cruse, but it's no good, she doesn't like them. Then the church where my father was buried sends a wise and sympathetic lady called Audrey. She hasn't got a degree in counselling or any performance measures to meet but my mother likes her straight away and Audrey comes round for the three sessions she is allowed to do; she has to move on after that, she explains. Everyone needs counselling; there is a long waiting list. People have lost faith in the church but they believe in the NHS and the NHS promises immortality, and then they can't cope with death.

The sessions seem to go well; I am hopeful when Audrey calls me after the last one.

"It's no good, dear," she says. "Your mother suffers from *inconsolable* grief. There is *nothing* that can be done."

And indeed, my mother's big eyes, of which she has always been so proud, always seem fixed and staring, gazing from person to person – where is he? Why aren't you him? Her mouth seems slightly open and rounded. Some years after she dies, I am visiting Oslo and I see in the Art Gallery Munch's *The Scream*, and I think, yes that's it. I understand; the two figures on the bridge are moving away into the darkness. It is a great primal howl about loss, bereavement and death.

Excessive grief, as Queen Victoria's family discovered, can be wearying. Eventually everyone backs off. We shore my mother up as well as we can. She cannot use a cheque book or a credit card; my father has always done everything. We arrange for all her bills to be paid by direct debit; we arrange for Ring and Ride to take her shopping; we take her to the speedbank; we arrange a variety of odd job men to come in and do the tasks my father used to do. She enjoys her weekly trips to Tesco; she enjoys her grandchildren's visits, she loves to watch TV and listen to the radio, and she lives for her weekly visits to the cemetery. And that's about it. Her grief will never be bankrupt till she has spent the last copper coin of her sorrow.

One April morning in 2015, she awakes feeling unwell. She often feels unwell and is depressed, she tells us, to the point where we don't notice anymore. She puts on her dressing gown and slippers, and makes her way downstairs to the telephone. Death comes to meet her at the foot of the stairs, where we find her later, sitting at the telephone, her head laid back against the wall, eyes closed, receiver in hand still poised to phone – who? One of us? The doctor? 999? It was instantaneous, says the coroner, a stroke or a blood clot. She never knew a thing.

My dear Uncle Albert is not at her funeral. He died two years previously. He had been a widower from the age of fifty-five, as Aunty Mary died at fifty of chronic arthritis. Janet and Jim are grown up by then. He lives alone in a neat house in Wolverhampton; kept immaculate (he was in the Navy). He works till he is sixty-five; in his retirement he works in his garden where he grows flowers and vegetables and he plays golf.

Since my aunt died, he has always had a rescue dog for company; the first is Brew, named after the beer, and then a jolly pair called Spick and Span. In his eighties, he has a little dog called Sunny. She is tiny, with short legs, and a tail that wags perpetually; she sits on my uncle's lap or shoulders, loving him.

He has a quadruple bypass when he is in his eighties, but he recovers well and goes to live with my cousin Janet for a bit. He has his own bedroom with a French window so Sunny can go out when she pleases.

Then, nearly aged ninety, he develops a wasting disease. Everything goes; sight, sound, smell, taste, touch. He becomes paralysed, immobile. Janet copes as long as she can, and then, weeping, she has to send him to the hospice. We want to visit him but Janet says no; he is too upset about how he is.

She does, just once, take Sunny to see him; they lift the little dog onto the bed, and she licks my uncle's face. Tears roll down his cheeks.

He dies on a bleak January morning, just as Janet is on her way to see him.

After the funeral, at the house, I see Sunny sitting waiting – waiting – waiting – at the door of my uncle's room.

I ask Janet what they are going to do with Sunny. Oh, keep her, she says, she was a part of Dad.

But Sunny dies only a few months later.

"Dead of a broken heart," says my cousin Janet. "She couldn't understand that he wasn't coming back."

They say that when you wake up at three o'clock in the morning, you should close your eyes and think of happy times.

I think a great deal of my University years; when thanks to the grants system I became the first family member to go to University. A whole new world. I make my best friends, friends for life; I am with other people who love literature as much as I do. I stop reading the *Daily Mirror* and take *The Guardian*. I discover theatre, opera and ballet.

Yet at other times, I shut my eyes tight, and imagine I am a little girl in a cotton frock, moving down a dark tunnel. I open the door at the end and enter into brilliant sunshine; Guildford St, Lozells, Birmingham in the 1960s. I run, as fast as I can, on my little girl's legs, to no 37, where my parents and my grandmother are waiting. It is the Sixties again, the decade when the Beatles sang and the sun came out and everyone smiled and was happy, and the world seemed full of hope.

Here comes the sun, it's all right ... the sun did come out and for a short time everything was all right.

USEFUL WEBSITES

http://www.astonbrook-through-astonmanor.co.uk/
http://www.birminghamhistory.co.uk/forum/index.php
http://www.lucasmemories.co.uk/site/index.html

On facebook:
Pics of Old Brum
This is Birmingham
UK Growing up in the 50s and 60s

*   *   *

In memory of:
Mom and Dad and Nan
Floss and Bert